Scotland's leading educational publishers

National 5
HISTORY
SUCCESS GUIDE

N5 HISTORY
SUCCESS GUIDE

Andrew Baxby, Denise Dunlop,
Neil McLennan, Thom Sherrington

© 2013 Leckie & Leckie Ltd
Cover image © Sergey Dolgikh

001/31102013

10 9 8 7 6 5 4 3 2 1

ISBN 9780007504923

Published by
Leckie & Leckie Ltd
An imprint of HarperCollins*Publishers*
Westerhill Road, Bishopbriggs, Glasgow, G64 2QT
T: 0844 576 8126   F: 0844 576 8131
leckieandleckie@harpercollins.co.uk   www.leckieandleckie.co.uk

Special thanks to
Roda Morrison (project management and copyedit); Alistair Coats (proofread); Ink Tank (cover design); Q2A Bill Smith (layout)

Printed in Italy by Lego, S.P.A.

A CIP Catalogue record for this book is available from the British Library.

Acknowledgements
We would like to thank the following for permission to reproduce photographs. Page numbers are followed, where necessary, by t (top), b (bottom), m (middle), l (left) or r (right).

P10t Jupiterimages, P10b SuperStock, P5 Getty Images, P10b John Opie, P13 Popperfoto/Getty Images, P17 © Scottish Life Archive, National Museums of Scotland. Licensor www.scran.ac.uk, P19 Reproduced with the permission of Strathclyde Partnership for Transport , P20 © Scottish Life Archive, National Museums of Scotland. Licensor www.scran.ac.uk, P21 © Hulton-Deutsch/ CORBIS, P22 Alphonse Leong / Shutterstock.com, P23 © The Art Archive/Superstock, P25m Getty Images, P26 Popperfoto/Getty Images, P29 Reproduced with the permission of Leeds University Library, P30 SSPL via Getty Images, P31 © Imperial War Museums (Q 20002), P33 © Scottish Life Archive, National Museums of Scotland. Licensor www.scran.ac.uk, P35 Millicent Fawcett - Getty Images, P35 Emmeline Pankhurt - Getty Images, P35 John Maclean - Getty Images, P38 British Library/Robana via Getty Images, P41 Getty Images, P43 English School, P51 National Records of Scotland, BR-FOR-4-34-223, P52 Lairich Rig, P54b Getty Images, P58 Getty Images, P60 © Scottish Life Archive, National Museums of Scotland. Licensor www.scran.ac.uk, P62 By Permission of People's History Museum, P64 Time & Life Pictures, P65t Getty Images, P65b Getty Images, P67 Alinari via Getty Images, P69 Getty Images, P70 Getty Images, P75t Popperfoto/Getty Images, P75b Bundesarchiv, Bild 183-R15068 / CC-BY-SA, P82 Getty Images, P83 Getty Images, P85b Time & Life Pictures/Getty Images, P86 NY Daily News via Getty Images, P89 Getty Images, P92 Getty Images, P95t Getty Images, P98 Time & Life Pictures/ Getty Images, P103 Gamma-Rapho via Getty Images, P104 Getty Images, P105 Nikita Khrushchev - Getty Images,

All other images from Shutterstock

Introduction

About this Success Guide

This guide is designed to help students achieve their potential in National 5 History. It should be used as part of the student's revision for the exam in terms of both content and skills.

The content is broken down into four sub-headings for each chapter and conforms to the SQA guidelines. This provides students with an easy-to-manage revision structure. The Exam skills section supports students when focusing on how to answer the exam questions. The Added Value Unit section gives suggestions for possible topics for study.

Who is this guide for?

This guide can be used by students at home and in class as part of their revision for the National 5 History exam. Parents may wish to use this guide in order to support students in their revision. Teachers may find the clear structure of the guide useful in order to plan more detailed lessons on each section.

How can this guide be used?

Students

The best way to revise using this guide is, first, to decide which topic you want to revise. Then set yourself a time limit and stick to it. For example, give yourself 15 minutes to revise one sub-heading (one double page). Do more than just read the information! Making your own notes as you go or turning the information into spider diagrams will help you retain the information. If there are parts you are unsure of, return to your class notes. When you are confident that you know the content of the sub-heading you should try the Quick Test at the bottom of the page. Also, look at the Top Tips, Think Points and Did You Know? sections. The biographies at the end of each section give you more insight into some of the key figures in the topic. This book should not just be used to 'cram' on the day of the exam, although there is no harm in one last read outside the exam hall!

When you have revised a whole topic you should think about doing some practice questions. Use the Exam skills section to help you with this. The Added Value Unit section should give you some ideas for a focus.

Parents

This guide will give you and your child an overview of the National 5 History course. While not exhaustive, it does contain the key points they will be studying in school and covers the main areas they will be examined on. The Quick Tests are a good way to help check your child's knowledge of the topic. The Exam skills section should give you an understanding of the expected standard for the exam. The Added Value Unit section gives some suggestions of topics for a focus. Each of the double page spreads covers one of the topics that your child will be examined on. A conversation with your child about what they are going to be examined on and what types of questions they are likely to be asked is a good starting point for using this book together. Each chapter also has Top Tips, Think Points, and Did You Know? sections, which aim to promote deeper learning.

Mary, from the 'Rough Wooing' to becoming Queen of France, to 1559

Scottish society in the 1540s

Scotland in the sixteenth century was a dangerous place and people's lives were hard.

- Most people lived in townships in the countryside. Their lives were controlled by local landowners.
- There were a growing number of burghs, centres for craftsmen and traders. Royal burghs were granted the privilege of trading overseas.
- The monarchy governed with the help of the Privy Council and Parliament. The monarch was advised by the nobility, important churchmen, officials and representatives of the royal burghs.
- Monarchs depended on the support of the nobility. Nobles ruled regions on behalf of the monarch and helped keep the peace. Nobles were expected to gather men to fight for the monarch in times of war. Regents were chosen from the nobility when Scotland did not have an adult monarch.

TOP TIP

Sometimes it is helpful to link key points to visual triggers in order to remember them. Illustrate these four key points on Scottish society in the 1540s. Look at your drawing a week later. Can you remember the key points?

The Scottish Church in the 1540s

Religion played a very important part in people's lives but there was growing criticism of the Catholic Church.

- The Church was too rich and did not use its wealth to help the poor.
- Some churchmen led wealthy lifestyles.
- Some churchmen held several church positions and often did not do their work properly.
- Some monks and nuns did not lead holy lives.
- Kings and nobles bought Church positions for family members.
- The Church was criticised for selling indulgences.
- Fewer people attended church and churches were falling into disrepair.

Laws were introduced to encourage churchmen to learn to read and to preach more often and there were laws against the sale of Church positions. These attempts at reform were unsuccessful.

Scotland's relationship with England and France

In 1542 Mary, Queen of Scots succeeded to the throne. As she was too young to rule herself, James Hamilton, Earl of Arran was made Regent of Scotland. In 1554 Mary's French mother, Mary of Guise, became Regent. During these years both the English and the French tried to gain control of Scotland.

- **The Treaty of Greenwich** (1543) arranged for Mary to marry Henry VIII's son, Edward. Henry insisted that Mary be sent to England. He also wanted control of Scottish castles south of the Forth. He seized Scottish ships and demanded that Scotland put an end to the old alliance with France.

- Henry's demands resulted in the Scottish Parliament cancelling the Treaty of Greenwich. Henry sent armies to punish the Scots and capture Mary. The English invasions were called the '**Rough Wooing**'.

- The English attacks led to the **Treaty of Haddington** in 1548. Mary was to go to France for safety and would marry the French king's son, Francis.

- In 1558 Mary and Francis were married. In 1559, on his father's death, Francis became king of France and Mary became queen.

- Mary's dynastic position became stronger in 1558 on the accession of Elizabeth I. Many Catholics did not recognise Protestant Elizabeth as the true Queen of England. Mary was Elizabeth's closest living relation and heir.

Mary and her first husband, Francis II of France

Quick Test

1. How did the nobility support the monarchy in the sixteenth century?
2. What criticisms were made of the Catholic Church in the sixteenth century?
3. Why did the Scottish Parliament cancel the Treaty of Greenwich?
4. Why was Mary, Queen of Scots sent to France in 1548?

The Reformation in Scotland, 1560

The growth of Protestantism in Scotland

In the 1540s and 1550s Protestant ideas began to spread. People began to follow the ideas of Martin Luther, a German monk who criticised the Catholic Church. Martin Luther's ideas spread in a movement called the Reformation.

- People began to protest against the corruption of the Catholic Church in Scotland.
- Religious pamphlets from Europe and English translations of the Bible began to appear.
- Reformers such as George Wishart began to spread Protestant ideas.
- John Knox, one of Wishart's followers, gained support for the reformed Church. Knox was influenced by John Calvin, a follower of Martin Luther.
- Calvin believed people should live strict lives to save them from damnation and also believed church services should be simple and be held in plain churches.
- In 1557 some Protestant Scottish lords declared their intention to establish the Reformation in Scotland in a document called the 'First band of the Lords of the Congregation of Christ'. They became known as the Lords of the Congregation.

THINK POINT

Knox wrote a pamphlet called *The First Blast of the Trumpet Against the Monstrous Regiment of Women*. Knox referred to females as 'frail, weak, feeble and impatient creatures'. This attack was aimed at Mary of Guise and Mary Tudor of England. How do you think Mary, Queen of Scots and Elizabeth I of England felt about Knox's views on female rulers?

Rebellion against Mary of Guise

In 1559 there was a rising against Mary of Guise. The reasons for this were:

- Mary, Queen of Scots' marriage increased French influence over Scotland. The marriage treaty stated that Scotland was now part of France, a Catholic country.
- Mary of Guise had Protestant leaders executed.
- The death of Mary Tudor in 1558 and the accession of Elizabeth, a Protestant, to the throne of England, encouraged Protestant leaders in Scotland.

The Protestant rebellion was supported by Elizabeth I while Mary of Guise received help from France. Fighting took place until the death of Mary of Guise in June 1560.

- The Treaty of Edinburgh in July 1560 agreed that both French and English forces were to withdraw from Scotland.
- The Scottish Parliament passed laws which led to Scotland becoming a Protestant country.

The Reformation after 1560

The regencies of Moray and Morton

The Protestant Reformation in Scotland developed under the regents who governed while James VI was too young to rule. In 1567 a law was passed stating that official positions were only to be held by Protestants. By 1574 most parishes had Protestant ministers and in 1579 Bibles began to be produced in Scotland. The Protestant Reformation was also strengthened after the defeat of the Queen's Lords in 1573 under Regent Morton.

Regent	Dates
Earl of Moray	1567–1570
Earl of Lennox	1570–1571
Earl of Mar	1571–1572
Earl of Morton	1572–1578

Young James VI

- Brought up Protestant, in the care of a strict tutor, George Buchanan.
- Became concerned by the power of the Protestant Church after being kidnapped by a group of Protestant lords led by Lord Ruthven (the Ruthven Raid, 1582).
- Wanted to have control of the Church through bishops; was opposed to presbyteries, i.e. church organisations made up of ministers and leading members of the church.

Andrew Melville and the development of Presbyterianism

The Protestant Reformation progressed further under the leadership of Andrew Melville. The Second Book of Discipline in 1578 contained his ideas for the Church in Scotland.

- Bishops should be abolished.
- The General Assembly should only consist of ministers and elders and not nobles or burgesses.
- The Kirk should have strict control of people's behaviour.

James VI as a boy

Quick Test

1. List five leading Protestant reformers mentioned in this chapter.
2. Who were the Lords of the Congregation?
3. Why was there a rising against Mary of Guise in 1559?
4. What was the Ruthven Raid?

Mary's reign, 1561–1567

Mary's return to Scotland

Mary, Queen of Scots returned to Scotland in August 1561. Most Scots welcomed Mary as Queen. She was young, beautiful and kind, and enjoyed light-hearted pastimes such as dancing at her court in Holyrood Palace in Edinburgh. Mary, however, was a Roman Catholic and faced problems in ruling a Protestant Scotland. These problems included:

- Some Scots opposed Mary as she was young and female.
- Some Scots resented Mary's French upbringing.
- Some Scots feared that Scotland would return to being Roman Catholic.

An etching depicting Mary's arrival in Leith, 1561

Mary's early reign

In the early years of her reign, Mary set up a successful government which included her Protestant half-brother James Stewart, who Mary made Earl of Moray. Mary travelled around Scotland to get to know her subjects and took action against nobles, such as the Earl of Huntly, who challenged her authority. Although she continued to practise the Catholic religion, Mary followed a tolerant religious policy.

- Mary allowed her Scottish subjects to follow the Protestant religion.
- Mary gave money to the Protestant Church.
- Mary did not allow priests to say Mass.
- Mary held several meetings with John Knox despite his criticism of her religion and lifestyle.

Mary's marriage

In 1565 Mary married Henry Stewart, Lord Darnley. This marriage caused problems for Mary and weakened her control of Scotland.

- Darnley was resented by many of the Scottish nobles. Mary's half-brother James, Earl of Moray, rebelled, which led to the Chaseabout Raid.
- Darnley's bad temper, drinking and long absences humiliated Mary.
- Darnley was involved in the murder of Mary's secretary, David Riccio, who was disliked due to his influence and friendship with Mary. He was also

The murder of Riccio

distrusted as he was a Catholic. Riccio was dragged from Mary's private rooms in Holyrood Palace and was stabbed 56 times with daggers and swords in front of Mary, who was pregnant at the time.

Darnley's murder in 1567 ultimately led to Mary's downfall. Darnley's Lodging house, Kirk O' Fields, was blown up by gunpowder and Darnley's body was found in the back garden. He had been suffocated. It was believed that a group of nobles including James Hepburn, Earl of Bothwell, and the Earl of Morton, were responsible.

TOP TIP

When looking at historical sources about Mary, Queen of Scots, consider the reliability of the evidence. Think about the authorship of the source. For example, sources written by John Knox, a Protestant leader, were biased against Mary.

Mary's hurried marriage to Bothwell led to Mary being blamed for Darnley's murder. Some people believed Mary was already in a relationship with Bothwell and that together they had plotted to murder Darnley. Mary's enemies now thought she was unfit to govern.

Rebellion against Mary

- Some Scottish nobles rebelled. Mary surrendered to the rebels at Carberry Hill on 15 June 1567.
- Mary was captured and imprisoned in Loch Leven Castle.
- Mary was forced to abdicate and her 13 month old son was crowned James VI. The Earl of Moray became Regent.
- Mary was imprisoned for ten and a half months but in May 1568 she managed to escape disguised as a servant with the help of her jailors.
- Mary raised an army at Hamilton but was defeated by the Earl of Moray's army on 13 May 1568, at the Battle of Langside.
- Mary fled to England in the hope that her cousin Elizabeth would help her.

Quick Test

1. What problems did Mary face when she returned to Scotland in 1561?
2. How did Mary show she was a strong ruler in the early years of her reign in Scotland?
3. Why was Riccio disliked by Darnley and the Scottish nobles?
4. Where was Mary imprisoned in Scotland after her surrender at Carberry Hill in June 1567?

Mary in England, 1567–1587

Mary's imprisonment

Mary escaped from her Scottish enemies but she did not receive help from Elizabeth. Instead Elizabeth had Mary imprisoned.

In 1568–1569 an enquiry was held to investigate Mary's involvement in Darnley's murder. The Earl of Moray produced a silver casket containing love letters Mary had allegedly written to Bothwell as evidence that they had plotted together to kill Darnley. The English nobles examining the letters could not decide if Mary was guilty or not. Elizabeth, however, saw Mary as a rival and kept Mary in captivity for almost 19 years. She was moved from one castle to another to prevent her supporters from plotting to free her.

Why did Mary's presence in England cause problems for Elizabeth?

- If Mary was sent back to Scotland, she might be executed by her Protestant enemies. Elizabeth would be acknowledging the right of subjects to rebel against their ruler.
- If Mary was sent abroad, Catholic rulers might use her as a focus to rally support for an attack against Protestant England.
- If Mary was allowed to live freely in England, she might try to seize the English throne. As Elizabeth was childless, she feared that Mary's supporters would try to kill her and put Mary on the English throne.
- Even if Mary remained imprisoned in England, she could still be a rallying point for English Catholics who believed that Mary, a Roman Catholic related to the English royal family, should be Queen of England. This became a real danger for Elizabeth in 1570 when the Pope declared Elizabeth was no longer England's rightful Queen.

Catholic plots

Mary's presence became an increasing threat to Elizabeth's position as Queen and to her safety, as Mary became the focus of Catholic plots to kill Elizabeth and to make Mary Queen of England. Mary knew little about many of the plots.

1569	The Northern Catholics	A group of Mary's supporters wanted Mary to succeed to the English throne and restore the Catholic religion.
1571	The Ridolfi Plot	Roberto Ridolfi, an Italian agent of the Pope, planned to use a Spanish army to free Mary and the Catholic Duke of Norfolk from the Tower of London. The plan involved Mary marrying Norfolk and becoming Queen of England.
1583	The Throckmorton Plot	A plan for a Spanish invasion of England.
1585	The Parry Plot	A plot to assassinate Elizabeth.
1586	The Babington Plot	Sir Anthony Babington, an English Catholic, plotted to free Mary, with Spanish help, murder Elizabeth and restore the Roman Catholic religion by placing Mary on the English throne.

However, Sir Francis Walsingham, one of Elizabeth's ministers, was appointed to find evidence against Mary. Mary's involvement in the Babington Plot provided the evidence that Mary was plotting against Elizabeth.

- Mary wrote to Babington agreeing to the plot.
- Unknown to Mary, a trap had been laid and all letters to and from Mary were being read by Walsingham.
- Mary was arrested and put on trial. Mary defended herself with dignity but was found guilty of treason and sentenced to death.

Mary's execution

Elizabeth hesitated to sign Mary's death warrant. Elizabeth was reluctant to kill another Queen and Mary was Elizabeth's cousin. On 1 February 1587 Elizabeth signed Mary's death warrant which had been hidden among a pile of letters requiring her signature. Elizabeth later claimed she signed the letters quickly without reading them properly. On 8 February 1587 Mary was executed in the Great Hall of Fotheringhay Castle.

THINK POINT

How many years did Mary spend in France? In Scotland? In England? In which country did she spend most of her time? Is this surprising? If so, think of a reason.

The execution of Mary

Quick Test

1. What was produced by the Earl of Moray as evidence that Mary and Bothwell had planned Darnley's murder?
2. Why was Mary moved from castle to castle during her imprisonment in England?
3. What was the Babington Plot?
4. How did Elizabeth eventually sign Mary's death warrant?

Timeline

1542 – Mary is born and becomes Queen of Scotland.

1543 – The Scottish Parliament agrees and then rejects the Treaty of Greenwich.

1548 – Treaty of Haddington. Mary leaves Scotland to live in France.

1554 – Mary of Guise becomes Regent.

1558 – Mary marries the Dauphin Francis.

1560 – Scotland becomes a Protestant country.

1561 – Mary returns to Scotland.

1567 – Darnley is murdered. Mary marries James, the Earl of Bothwell.

1568 – Mary escapes from Loch Leven Castle and flees to England. Mary is imprisoned in England.

1587 – Mary is executed at Fotheringhay Castle.

Biographies

Henry Stewart, Lord Darnley (1545–1567)

Darnley and Mary were married in July 1565. He was Mary's cousin and, like Mary, had a claim to the English throne. Darnley, however, was not a good husband to Mary and his ambitions to be crowned King of Scotland made him many enemies. He was murdered in February 1567.

James Hepburn, Earl of Bothwell (1534–1578)

Bothwell and Mary were married in May 1567. The marriage led to an uprising by the Scottish nobles who believed Bothwell was guilty of Darnley's murder. After the surrender of Mary's army at Carberry Hill, Bothwell fled to Scandinavia in the hope of raising support for Mary but was imprisoned in Denmark and died in captivity in 1578.

John Knox (1514–1572)

In 1547 John Knox was sent to row in the French galleys as a punishment for joining the murderers of Cardinal Beaton, in St Andrew's castle. After his release, Knox studied Protestant ideas on the Continent before returning to Scotland in 1559. In 1560 his Book of Discipline outlined his ideas for the reformed Church in Scotland.

David Riccio (1533–1566)

David Riccio came to Scotland in 1561 and became Mary's secretary in 1564. Mary and Riccio shared a love of music and poetry but their close friendship led to his murder by a group of Scottish nobles in March 1566.

James Douglas, Earl of Morton (1516–1581)

James Douglas became Regent in 1572. He ended the conflict with Mary's supporters. In 1580 he was arrested for his involvement in Darnley's murder and executed in Edinburgh in 1581. He was beheaded on the maiden, a guillotine he himself had introduced into Scotland.

Immigration to Scotland

Why did immigrants come to Scotland?

From 1830 to 1939, Scotland witnessed the arrival of immigrants from across Europe. Each arrived for a variety of reasons. These can be divided into 'push' and 'pull' factors.

Immigration and emigration, to 1939

Push	Pull
High unemployment rates in Europe and Ireland.	Job opportunities created by the industrial revolution.
Wages were often very low in these areas.	Scotland offered higher wages for the immigrants.
Religious and political persecution (especially Jews and Catholics from eastern Europe). Many Jews fled central Europe to escape the Nazis.	Scotland was seen as a place where different religious practices were more accepted, and democracy ruled.
The potato famine in Ireland forced people to leave due to the threat of starvation.	Scotland was near to Ireland and offered work and food to the hungry Irish workers.
	Scotland was also a stop on the way to America (especially for eastern Europeans).

Where did the immigrants settle?

> ### TOP TIP
> **E**migration = leaving (remember the 'E' in exit). **I**mmigration = arriving (remember the 'I' in into). Often pull factors and push factors are closely related. For example, low wages are a push factor and better wages are a pull factor.

In general, immigrants settled in the central belt, where the jobs were.

Irish immigrants arrived desperately seeking employment and often worked as navvies, building the canals, railways and roads. Glasgow and Dundee became swamped with Irish immigrants.

Jewish immigrants tended to settle on the south side of Glasgow, working as professionals (lawyers, accountants, bankers). Their religious practices often seemed bizarre to the native Scots and they found it difficult to integrate into Scottish society.

In general, Jews were seen as less of an economic threat than the Irish, as unemployment was low in the Jewish community.

Italians generally came to escape the crushing poverty in Italy's rural communities. Many used Scotland as a stop-off on the way to America. They set up ice cream parlours and coffee shops. Italians faced hostility when Mussolini sided with Hitler in the Second World War.

An ice cream parlour, Edinburgh, 1907

What was the impact of Empire on Scotland?

- There were opportunities to work for the Colonial Government or army, which helped some become very rich.
- The opportunities for Scots to emigrate to far-flung places helped to relieve some of the problems at home. There was less pressure on the scarce farmland of the western Highlands, and widespread starvation was avoided.
- Unemployment in the towns and cities was lessened.
- Profits made by Scottish businessmen in the Empire helped Glasgow's city fathers to supply clean water, affordable gas, public parks and better sewerage.
- New materials and foodstuffs arrived. Glasgow became the 'second city of the Empire' with ships built there going all over the world. Trains built in Scotland were running on the new lines in Canada, India and New Zealand. Jute from India gave Dundee factories material to work with.

Politically, the Empire arguably gave Scotland a higher profile in the world, and the export of 'Scottishness' to many parts of the Empire gives an idea of the influence that the Empire had on Scotland.

However, some have argued that this emigration led to a 'brain drain'. Many of the finest businessmen and thinkers left Scotland to make their fortunes in the Empire.

Quick Test

1. List three push and three pull factors for migration to Scotland.
2. Why were Jewish immigrants seen as less of a threat than other immigrants?
3. Why did Jewish immigration increase in the 1930s?
4. What was the name given to Glasgow at the height of the Empire?

Experience of immigrants, 1880s–1939

Where did the immigrants live and work?

Many of the immigrants to Scotland lived in the poorest conditions. They worked in the poorest paid jobs and so could not afford better accommodation.

They were often employed in dangerous, dirty work such as in factories or coal mines. Due to their willingness to work for low wages, they were accused of stealing jobs as many employers would sack well-paid Scots and employ low-paid immigrants.

A miner at Camp Colliery, Motherwell, circa 1890

Irish immigration

TOP TIP

Sectarianism (religious tension) was often a symptom of the economic problems and high unemployment rate at the time. Tension increased at times of hardship.

In Scotland, the Protestant Irish tended to integrate well into all areas of society, whereas Catholics remained on the margins of society. There was racial/sectarian tension in certain areas of Scotland, and this increased at times of unemployment. The experiences of the Protestant Irish and Catholic Irish differed in various ways:

Catholics	Protestants
Made up about 75% of all Irish immigrants.	Made up about 25% of all Irish immigrants.
Had more in common with the Scottish Highlanders and spoke Gaelic.	Had more in common with the Scottish Lowlanders and spoke English.
Religion marked them out as very different from the establishment.	Formed Orange Lodges in order to preserve their way of life and to show their rejection of the Catholic religion.
To begin with, they integrated well by marrying Scots, changing surnames and religion.	Integrated more easily as they had more in common politically, and they often had Scottish sounding surnames.
Found it difficult to find employment in certain areas – were sometimes paid less than Protestants.	Often found it easier to gain employment.

As numbers of Catholic immigrants grew, so did the native Scots' resentment. Catholics tended to remain in their own communities and were increasingly blamed for the high unemployment. Many were happy to work for low wages and live in very poor conditions. This made them easy targets to blame for the ever-worsening living conditions in Scotland's growing towns. A common myth was that the Irish Catholics were coming to Scotland in order to seek Poor Relief.

In the 1920s there was significant violence between Catholics and Protestants in Glasgow and other parts of Scotland. However, tension in Scotland should not be exaggerated, as throughout the nineteenth century there are examples of co-operation, such as in the building of the canals, railways and ships. During the First World War, Catholics and Protestants fought side-by-side in the British Forces.

What was the impact of Irish immigration on Scotland?

Irish immigration had a very mixed impact on Scotland.

- The Irish navvies helped establish Scotland's transport infrastructure, building roads, railways and canals. For example, in 1890 the Glasgow subway was tunnelled using largely Irish labourers.
- The arrival of a large (and cheap) workforce from Ireland did help boost the economy, even if Scots workers were unemployed as a result.
- The arrival of thousands of Irish Catholics led to the establishment of a separate system of Catholic schools.
- Sports teams were set up as a focus for young immigrant men; for example, Celtic, Hibernian and Dundee Hibernian (now Dundee United) football clubs were founded.
- Politically, Irish workers played a large role in the rise of the Labour Party.

Opening of the Glasgow subway, 1896

Quick Test

1. Why were Irish Catholic immigrants often unpopular in Scotland?
2. Why were Protestants accepted more quickly?
3. Give two lasting impacts of Catholic immigration.
4. What did Irish navvies help to build?

Scottish emigration, 1830s–1939

While there were large numbers arriving in Scotland at this time, there was also significant **emigration** *from* Scotland.

Poverty was a key factor in pushing people from Scotland. We know this as emigration peaked in the 1850s, 1870s, early 1900s and between the World Wars. These coincided with periods of significant economic hardship.

Why did Scots leave?

Jobs

In the 1870s farming experienced a downturn due to foreign competition. Thousands lost their jobs and they and their families went hungry. In the 1900s fishing was also hit hard by foreign competition. The slump after the First World War and the Great Depression saw heavy industry go into decline, forcing those in the cities to leave and find work.

Highland Clearances

Some were forced from the land due to the Highland Clearances. The growth in population of the nineteenth century meant that the land could not feed the people living there. The crofts were getting smaller and rents were increasing drastically. Landlords realised they could make more money from the land by grazing sheep (especially when the value of wool rose) and from creating shooting estates. To make matters worse, the potato famine of 1846 left 150 000 people at risk of starvation.

An evicted family in Lochmaddy, 1895

Thus, people were keen to move away from the poor conditions of the Highlands, but they were also forced to move by ruthless landlords.

The Church

Some were encouraged to move abroad by the opportunities of missionary work. The Presbyterian Church gave Scots clergy the opportunity to venture to exciting places in the Empire. They were supported financially to set up missions in order to convert natives and other migrants to Christianity. Missionaries, such as Mary Slessor (Nigeria), Alexander Duff (India) and William Chalmers Burns (China) continued to spread the Scottish Presbyterian message far and wide and encouraged others to follow.

Other organisations

Others were encouraged to move by the many emigration societies and the Colonial Government. Emigration societies offered support to (mostly skilled) workers in terms of transport costs and finding employment. This was especially common in Canada. They advertised for workers and organised everything for the migrant, even providing land for farming in the country of destination.

The Colonial Land and Emigration Commissioners gave grants and loans to support emigrants in the New World. After the Empire Settlement Act of 1922, the government gave money to countries of the Empire in order to encourage emigration. The New Zealand and Australian governments offered free travel for those working in domestic service.

The attraction of the New World

Some moved due to the pull of the 'New World', i.e. Canada, Australia, New Zealand and the USA. Wages tended to be higher, there was more land to farm and more jobs to be had in the cities. They could start again in a country with better farmland and more freedom. The land tended to be very cheap and many Scots set up huge plantations and ranches. Others moved in order to join family already successfully established. Others still were lured away from the sectarian problems at home by the idea of religious freedom.

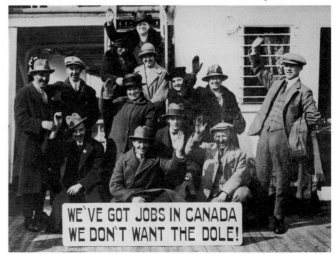

Thus, Scots moved for a wide variety of reasons; some were pushed, others were pulled.

A group of Scots leaving for Canada, 1925

Quick Test

1. Why did the Highland Clearances happen?
2. What was the role of the church in Scottish emigration?
3. Why is 1922 important to the story?
4. Where is the New World?

Experience of Scots abroad, 1830s–1939

Where did Scots settle?

Scots moved to a variety of locations across the globe including England, but the most common destinations were Canada, Australia, New Zealand and India. Even today, the Scottish influence can be seen in these countries.

Canada

More Scots went to Canada than anywhere else before 1847. They proved very successful in industry, dominating textiles, paper, sugar, oil, iron, coal, steel, furniture making, the fur trade and banking. They also had a huge influence on culture. Scots formed Burns clubs and Caledonian societies, and introduced rugby, football and curling. They played a huge role in politics, and Scots were key in making sure that Canada's main language was English and not French. John A Macdonald (from Glasgow) was Canada's first Prime Minister and founded the Canadian Mounted Police. There are lots of Scottish place names to this day (e.g. Dundee, Leith, Glasgow, Inverness, Stirling).

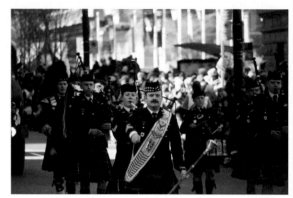
A pipe band in Vancouver, 2013

Australia

Scots were attracted to Australia in large numbers from 1851 with the discovery of gold. Scots were mostly successful in industries such as the wool trade, coal mining, farming, banking and construction.

The Presbyterian Church had a very strong hold in Australia. This was linked closely with the development of the education system.

However, Scots had a very negative impact on native societies, exemplified by the Warrigal Creek massacre. Aboriginal children were forcibly removed from their parents to be educated and westernised.

New Zealand

DID YOU KNOW?

The first recorded European settler in New Zealand was Scottish. His name was George Bruce. Use the internet to research more about some of these key Scots. Make a profile of each one, looking at where they came from, why they emigrated and what they achieved.

The New Zealand tourist board boasts that 'you'll find a Scottish presence everywhere in New Zealand life'. It was a popular destination for Scots (especially Otago), with a similar climate and terrain. Farming was the main industry for Scots in New Zealand, although they played an important role in banking, gold prospecting and skilled trades like shipbuilding. Caledonian Societies were very common, and Gaelic was the first language in some areas until the 1880s. Highland gatherings and St Andrew's societies flourished. Countless names show the impact of Scots (e.g. Clyde, Ben Nevis, Aviemore).

Again, the strong Presbyterian influence was exported. The 'Scotch Church' is still powerful to this day in Otago.

India

The British East India Company gave Scots the opportunity to trade with India, and they took full advantage. They flourished in the jute trade and Thomas Lipton was a shining example of the spirit of the Scots that ventured to this new land. He was a grocer and tea importer, who revolutionised tea drinking in Britain by making it cheaper and more fashionable.

Seven of the 12 viceroys of India were Scots, and they played crucial roles in all areas of government in the colony. They built railways, increased civil rights and encouraged female education. The relationship with native societies was generally more positive than elsewhere, although the Colonial Government did little to aid famine and suffering.

Lipton's tea being carried on elephants

Quick Test

1. How do we know that the impact of Scots in Canada was great and lasting?
2. Why did so many Scots go to Australia after 1851?
3. Where was the biggest Scottish settlement in New Zealand?
4. What did Thomas Lipton do?

Timeline

1833 – Mechanical spinning makes Dundee centre of world jute trade

1845 – Start of potato famine in Ireland

1846 – Potato famine affects the Highlands of Scotland

1851 – Gold discovered in Australia

1858 – India becomes a British colony

1867 – British North America formed (modern day Canada)

1875 – Hibernian Football Club formed by Irish born football enthusiasts

1901 – Modern day Australia formed as a Dominion in the British Empire

1907 – New Zealand becomes a Dominion in the British Empire

1922 – Government offers money to colonies to encourage emigration (Empire Settlement Act)

Biographies

Andrew Carnegie (1835–1919)

Born in Dunfermline, Carnegie made his name in America. His family emigrated to Pennsylvania in 1848, where he worked in a factory. He made his fortune in the railway expansion of the 1860s and 1870s. In the 1880s Carnegie formed steel companies that made him incredibly wealthy. His company was ultimately bought out for a vast sum of money. He spent his retirement funding projects in America, Scotland and elsewhere, including giving $10 million to Scotland's universities.

John Buchan, 1st Baron Tweedsmuir (1875–1940)

Brought up in Kirkaldy in Fife, Buchan led a fairly privileged life. He was well-educated and served in the diplomatic service after university. He went on to fight in the First World War and to become Governor General of Canada in 1935. He was also a famous author (*The Thirty-nine Steps* is his most famous work) and was a strong critic of the policy of appeasement in the 1930s.

Andrew Fisher (1862–1928)

Fisher was born in East Ayrshire and worked in a coal mine from age 10. When he lost his job in 1885 he decided to emigrate to Australia. There he again worked in mines and was elected as an MP for the Labour Party. He went on to be Prime Minister of Australia three times between 1908 and 1915. He was also High Commissioner to the UK between 1916 and 1921. He died in London of severe influenza in 1928. He was also suffering from dementia.

John Muir (1838–1914)

Born near Dunbar in East Lothian, Muir is considered the 'Father of the National Parks' in America. He is credited with preserving Yosemite and Sequoia National Parks. His name is given to numerous important places, but it is the 211-mile hiking trail in the Sierra Nevada mountain range in California that is probably the best-known. The John Muir award in the UK is given to those that complete wilderness and conservation challenges.

Thomas Lipton (1850–1931)

Tommy Lipton grew up in Glasgow's Gorbals area. He left school at 10, and set up his first market stall in 1870. He set up a business exporting tea from India and Ceylon (now Sri Lanka) in the 1890s. Lipton's plan was to reduce its cost and make it affordable for the average British shopper. His other novel idea was to begin packaging it, instead of selling it loose from the chest. He was knighted by Queen Victoria in 1898.

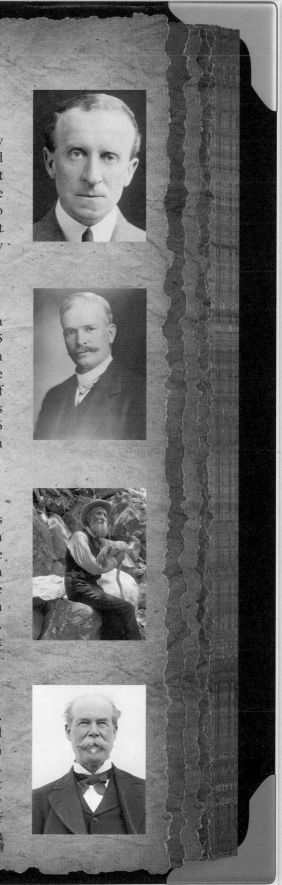

Scots on the Western Front

In 1914 war broke out between the Triple Alliance (Germany, Austria-Hungary, Italy) and the Triple Entente (Britain, France, Russia). Scots fought predominantly on the 'Western Front', which ran from the Belgian North Sea coast to the Franco-Swiss border.

TOP TIP

Research the involvement of Scots in major battles of the First World War. 30 000 Scottish troops fought at the battle of Loos and five soldiers were later awarded the Victoria Cross for bravery.

Why did so many Scots join the army?

Scots volunteered in massive numbers and many lied about their age to do so. As well as patriotism, there were other reasons for joining up:

Excitement	The war was portrayed as exciting and glamorous. The prevailing attitude was that it 'would be over by Christmas', so volunteers did not expect a long period of service.
Propaganda	Accusations of German atrocities in Belgium, e.g. rape of nuns, murder of babies and torture of civilians, were accepted as truth.
Football supporters	Thirteen players from the team 'Heart of Midlothian' volunteered to fight, which encouraged hundreds of supporters and other teams to follow suit.
Employment and wages	The average army pay of nine or ten shillings a week was more than many Scots were paid in civilian life.

Life in the trenches

Conditions in the trenches were horrific.

- Men often had to stand in mud up to their ankles. This led to diseases such as trench foot.
- Pests such as rats and lice were everywhere.
- Food was not nutritious (e.g. canned stew). Fresh fruit and vegetables were rare.
- Constant shellfire led to 'shell shock'.
- The danger of death was always close. Artillery fire was constant and enemy snipers could easily shoot men who stuck their heads above the parapet.

Conditions in the trenches could be terrible, with mud a particular problem.

New technology

The war evolved into a stalemate, so both sides dug trenches to defend their positions. This meant that traditional tactics such as the cavalry charge became obsolete. New technology was important in trying to break the stalemate.

Artillery	• Most widely used method of attack was heavy artillery fire. • Huge guns fired shells packed with explosives towards the enemy lines.
Gas	• Three main gases were used: mustard, chlorine and phosgene. • Effects varied from severe skin irritation to suffocation and death. • Proved to be unreliable because wind could blow it back towards the side it had come from; gas masks were developed to counter the effects.
Tanks	• Developed to advance into enemy territory, break through enemy barbed wire and clear the way for infantry to follow. • First used at the Battle of the Somme. • Often broke down and became stuck in the mud.
Machine guns	• The ultimate defensive weapon. • Two or three machine gunners could fire hundreds of rounds a minute into advancing enemy infantry.
Aircraft	• Initially used for reconnaissance missions over enemy territory. • Were later developed with machine guns attached to fire upon enemy aircraft.

Military tactics

British troops have been described as 'Lions led by donkeys' because, although they displayed great courage, the strategy of the British generals led to massive casualties.

The main tactic was to bombard the enemy with artillery fire and then send troops 'over the top' towards enemy lines. The German machine guns, however, easily slaughtered the advancing British troops. The Scottish General Douglas Haig, Commander of the British forces during the war, has been heavily criticised for persisting with this tactic when it was so expensive in human life. Others argue that his strategy exhausted the German army and was ultimately responsible for the British victory.

Quick Test

1. Why did so many Scots volunteer for the army?
2. Why did new technology play such an important role in the war?
3. What was the main tactic employed by the British forces?
4. Who led the British forces in the war?

Domestic impact of war: society and culture

The First World War has been described as a 'total war' because its effects were felt in the homes and workplaces of Britain and Scotland, not just on the battlefield.

Rationing

In 1914 Britain relied on imports for the majority of its food. Germany launched submarine attacks on British merchant ships to reduce Britain to the point of starvation. By 1917 there were food shortages, which led to rising prices and panic buying. This led to the introduction of rationing on items such as sugar, meat and butter. Some items remained rationed until 1920.

Changing role of women

The war is often seen as a turning point in the role of women in British society.
- As men left for the front, women filled the gaps in the workforce.
- Women worked on buses, as typists, in the civil service and in the police.
- Over 30 000 women worked in the munitions industry in Scotland and thousands joined the Women's Land Army, which helped to sustain agriculture.

It is argued that by proving that they could be relied upon to work, they also proved that they could be trusted to vote and play a prominent role in society.

However, at the end of the war most women lost their jobs and were expected to return to their pre-war roles. It can thus be argued that the role of the war in changing the role of women in society has been exaggerated.

Propaganda

Propaganda was political advertising used by the government to influence the way people thought about the war. The huge volume of propaganda meant that the war infiltrated every aspect of public life. It was used to:
- encourage Scots to enlist
- encourage Scots to ration food
- boost morale and increase public support for the war.

Conscription

After the initial rush of volunteers had waned the government was forced to introduce conscription to ensure army numbers remained adequate. Conscription meant that men were forced to join the army by law. In January 1916 the Military Service Act introduced conscription for single men aged 18–40. This was extended to married men in March 1916 and men up to 50 years old in 1918.

Conscientious objectors

Some men claimed they could not fight because they objected to the war on the grounds of conscience, citing their religious or political beliefs. 16 000 men in total were classified as conscientious objectors (COs or Conchies). Most COs agreed to do some sort of work to help the war effort, for example farm work, but absolutists refused to do anything to help the war effort and were sentenced to hard labour. One labour camp was situated in Dyce, on the outskirts of Aberdeen, and the men were forced to work in a granite quarry.

Conscientious objectors at Dyce Camp, near Aberdeen in 1916.

Casualties and deaths

The true number of Scots killed in the First World War will never be known. The official number given was 75 000, but some claim that a more accurate figure may be closer to 150 000. What is not debated is that almost every community in Scotland suffered devastating losses and a whole generation of men was lost.

TOP TIP

You can commemorate the losses suffered by your community by visiting your local war memorial. This will record the name and rank of the men who died in the First and Second World Wars.

Quick Test

1. What is a 'total war'?
2. What role did women play during the war?
3. What is propaganda?
4. On what grounds did conscientious objectors refuse to fight in the war?

Domestic impact of war: industry and economy

As well as having a major impact on the society and culture of Scotland, the Great War also impacted greatly on industry and the economy. Prior to the war the traditional heavy industries of shipbuilding, mining and metalwork were in decline. This was reversed during the war and unemployment virtually disappeared. Once peace was achieved, however, the old problems returned, unemployment rose and the economy suffered.

War work

Several industries were boosted thanks to the war. The Royal Navy took control of the main shipbuilding firms on the Clyde. Increased demand for ships boosted employment in the area. The jute industry in Dundee also thrived. Jute was used to make cloth for sandbags, which were in heavy demand to line the walls of the trenches. As the German naval blockade took effect and food imports became scarce, Scottish agriculture increased to meet the shortfall. Many Scots found employment in munitions factories, which kept the army supplied with weapons and shells.

The cordite explosive factory at Gretna provided employment for over 9000 women during World War I.

Reserved occupations

Under the 1916 Military Service Act one of the grounds for exemption was: 'If it is expedient in the national interests that (a man) should be engaged in other work, or, if he is being educated or trained for any other work, that he should continue.' This meant that men employed in industries essential to the war effort such as coal mining, shipbuilding and munitions were able to apply for exemption from service. There was no specified list of occupations, however – local tribunals decided each case individually.

Post-war decline of heavy industry

Unfortunately the boom that heavy industries experienced during the war did not last and in the post-war period there was a rise in unemployment and a fall in the economy.

One of the main reasons for this was that the war created a huge demand for ships, coal, metal, munitions and other essential items. Once the war ended there was no longer a need to support the war effort so these orders disappeared.

Furthermore, during the four years of the war Britain's trading partners were forced to look elsewhere for suppliers. Britain's traditional industries such as textiles, coal mining, steel and iron production now faced many global competitors. Post-war British exports fell by 20%. Scotland, which relied heavily on traditional industries for employment, was badly affected by this depression.

Shipbuilding was once a major employer in Glasgow but it, along with many other heavy industries, declined in the 1920s.

New industry in the 1920s

There was some growth of new industries in Britain in the 1920s. The motor industry, chemical industry and electric industry all grew during this time. However, these industries tended to be based in the Midlands or in the South of England and so did not benefit Scots, who found themselves unemployed due to the post-war depression. Many Scots were forced to emigrate to find work abroad.

THINK POINT

The First World War had a massive impact on society in Scotland, Britain and the whole world. Create a mind map showing all of the changes and events that it can be said to have had a direct impact upon. Start off by using the notes from this chapter, but then think about all of the other topics you have studied in History and add them too.

Quick Test

1. What was the effect of the outbreak of war on the Scottish economy?
2. Which industries received a boost from the war?
3. Why did the economy decline after the war?
4. Why did the new industries of the 1920s not benefit Scots?

Domestic impact of war: politics

Campaigns for women's suffrage

Prior to the war the peaceful suffragists and the militant suffragettes had been campaigning for the right of women to vote. When war broke out, however, both groups suspended their campaigns and supported the war effort. The suffragettes had been very active in Scotland, but postponed their campaigns at the outset of war.

Defence of the Realm Act (DORA)

The First World War led to the passing of the Defence of the Realm Act in 1914. This gave the government wide-ranging powers to legislate on people's lives to ensure the successful continuation of the war effort.

- Pub opening hours were cut and the strength of beer was weakened to ensure high production levels in industrial areas.

- DORA gave the government the power to take over factories and turn them into munitions works.

- It allowed the government to censor the press to avoid stories that they thought might damage public morale.

Before DORA the philosophy of successive governments had been 'laissez-faire', i.e. they did not want to interfere in people's lives. With the passing of DORA, however, the government actively legislated on many aspects of public life.

DID YOU KNOW?

The pub opening hours were most rigorously enforced in areas near to munitions factories. Previously pubs had opened at 5am and workers often used to stop in on their way to work. Disasters caused by drunkenness were a serious concern!

Extension of the franchise

- In 1914 only 60% of men over the age of 21, and no women, could vote.

- In 1918 the Representation of the People Act enfranchised all men over the age of 21 (19 if they had fought in active service) and 'respectable' women over the age of 30.

- The act gave the vote to 21 million extra people in Britain; 8·4 million were women.

- Many women saw this as a victory, but others were dissatisfied with the continued inequality. It was not until 1928 that women were granted the vote on an equal basis.

Rent strikes

Industrial areas in Scotland, especially around Glasgow, experienced a large increase in population as people moved there for work. This led to an increased demand for housing. Landlords capitalised on this increased demand by raising rents and evicting those who could not pay in favour of those that could. Many of those affected were women whose men were away fighting.

Crowds of striking workers gathered in George Square in 1919.

- In 1915 the Glasgow Housing Association was formed and began protesting against the unfair and expensive rents.
- Eventually 25 000 workers from all over Scotland went on strike, threatening major disruption to the war effort.
- The Rent Restriction Act, which froze rents at 1914 levels, was eventually passed.

Glasgow became known as 'Red Clydeside' because of the amount of political and industrial unrest. Politicians were genuinely scared that a socialist revolution could occur and in 1919 even sent army tanks to disperse protestors in George Square.

Homes for heroes

David Lloyd George promised that returning soldiers would have clean and sanitary homes ('Homes for heroes'). This idea came to mean more than a home to live in, but also a right to a better standard of living. The 1919 Housing Act promised funding for 500 000 homes. Unfortunately the unemployment and economic hardship of the 1920s made providing all of these houses impossible and only 213 000 were built.

Further acts passed in the inter-war years, however, meant that in total 1·1 million homes were built by local housing associations.

Quick Test

1. What was the impact of DORA?
2. Why did living conditions decline in Glasgow during the war?
3. What political changes occurred after the war ended?
4. How many new homes were built after the war?

Timeline

4 August 1914	– Britain declares war on Germany.
8 August 1914	– Defence of the Realm Act (DORA) passed.
25 September 1915	– First day of the Battle of Loos, in which 30 000 Scots fought.
10 December 1915	– Douglas Haig appointed Commander in Chief of the British forces.
27 January 1916	– Conscription introduced in Britain (Military Service Act).
1 July 1916	– First day of the Battle of the Somme. Britain suffered 60 000 casualties. This remains the worst day in the history of the British Army.
7 December 1916	– David Lloyd George becomes Prime Minister.
6 February 1918	– Representation of the People Act passed.
11 November 1918	– Armistice signed officially ending the First World War.

Biographies

Sir Douglas Haig (1861–1928)

Born in Edinburgh, Haig was appointed Commander in Chief of the British forces in 1915. His tactics have been blamed for the huge casualty rates among British soldiers, particularly at the Battle of the Somme, where the British Army suffered 60 000 casualties on the first day of fighting alone. In his retirement he set up and devoted his life to the Royal British Legion, which cares for ex-servicemen.

David Lloyd George (1863–1945)

A prominent Liberal politician, Lloyd George became Prime Minister in 1916 and held that post until 1922. Brought up in a working-class family in Wales, he was an influential social reformer. During the war it is even said he insisted the Royal Family use candles instead of electric lights during banquets to save power for the war effort.

Millicent Fawcett (1847–1929)

Leader of the National Union of Women's Suffrage Societies, otherwise known as the 'suffragists'. The suffragists believed in 'peaceful persuasion' and campaigned for the right to vote for women by holding rallies, publishing pamphlets and working with politicians. In 1914 she called off the suffrage campaign and encouraged women to contribute to the war effort.

Emmeline Pankhurst (1858–1928)

Along with her two daughters, Christabel and Sylvia, Emmeline Pankhurst was the founder and leader of the Women's Social and Political Union, otherwise known as the 'suffragettes'. Like the suffragists, the suffragettes wanted votes for women, but they favoured using militant protests to achieve their aims. At the outbreak of war they too postponed their campaigns and encouraged men to enlist and women to serve the war effort.

John Maclean (1879–1923)

A Scottish school teacher and revolutionary socialist, John Maclean was one of the leading figures of Red Clydeside. He protested vehemently against the First World War and was imprisoned many times. His actions during Red Clydeside made him a hero in Russia, where he even appeared on postage stamps.

The triangular trade

The nature of the slave trade

Slavery is thousands of years old and the buying and selling of slaves had been taking place in Africa for hundreds of years. The slave trade of the eighteenth century, however, was a new kind of slavery.

Reasons why the slave trade was different	Evidence
The Atlantic slave trade was on a much larger scale than ever before.	Millions of African people were transported across the Atlantic as slaves.
The slave trade was racist.	Only African people were captured and sold into slavery for life.
Slaves became the property of slave owners.	Slaves were regarded as goods rather than as people. Few slaves were given their freedom. The children of slaves also became slaves.
The slave trade was a cruel form of slavery.	Slaves were ill-treated and kept in inhuman conditions. The law allowed a slave owner to beat a slave to death.

The slave trade expanded after many European countries set up colonies in the New World of the Americas. Britain played a major part in the Atlantic slave trade between 1770 and 1807.

The organisation of the slave trade

The trading system known as the **triangular trade** started in Europe and often involved three separate voyages:

Stage One: Outward Passage

In the first stage ships sailed from a port such as Liverpool, Bristol or London to the coast of West Africa loaded with goods such as guns, alcohol, pots and pans and textiles to exchange for captured Africans. Industries supplying the slave traders, shipbuilding and the direct involvement in trading slaves made many individuals very wealthy in ports such as Liverpool and Bristol.

When the slave ships arrived on the African coast, British merchants would trade for slaves. Captured Africans, marched to the coast by African traders, were imprisoned in slave forts called 'factories' until the arrival of the slave ships.

- The slave trade had a devastating effect on West Africa. Europeans encouraged African states to go to war with one another so there would be more prisoners of war to sell as slaves. The population declined and traditional ways of life disappeared.

- Some African states such as the Dahomey and the Ashanti became very powerful due to their participation in the slave trade.

Stage Two: Middle Passage

The second stage was the transportation of enslaved Africans across the Atlantic Ocean to the Americas. This stage is known as the **Middle Passage**.

For most slaves the Middle Passage was an unbearable and brutal experience. Slaves were tightly packed and chained below deck in filthy, unsanitary conditions. Many slaves died from disease.

At the end of the Middle Passage, slaves were cleaned and made to look younger and healthier to make them more profitable. The slaves were then sold to plantation owners at auctions or 'scrambles'.

TOP TIP

Atlantic slave trade journeys often had three parts which made a triangular shape, linking three continents – Europe, Africa and the Americas – it was commonly called the 'triangular trade'. But not all slave voyages were triangular; some slave traders made single voyages.

Stage Three: Inward Passage

The third stage was the journey back to Europe with plantation-grown goods, such as rum, tobacco, coffee, sugar, molasses and cotton bought from the profits of selling African slaves to the plantation owners. The raw materials would be turned into manufactured goods in Britain and then sold for large profits in Europe.

The triangular trade could take almost a year from start to finish. There were many risks but large profits could be made at each point of the triangular trade.

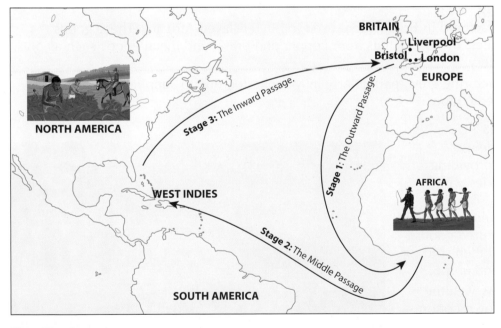

The triangular trade

Quick Test

1. What was new about the slave trade of the eighteenth century?
2. Describe conditions for slaves during the Middle Passage.
3. What were the three destinations in the triangular trade?
4. What goods were transported in the triangular trade?

Britain and the Caribbean

The effects of the Atlantic slave trade on Britain

The Atlantic slave trade had a major impact on Britain's economic prosperity and her people. Profits from the slave trade led to the growth of major ports and cities and played an important part in turning Britain into a wealthy industrial country. The slave trade also provided employment for thousands of people and many individuals gained power and wealth.

Tropical crops

- The climate and land in the New World colonies were suited to the growing of luxury crops such as sugar, cotton, coffee and tobacco. Britain made large profits, particularly from the trade in sugar which became very popular with British people.

Navigation

- The slave trade contributed to the growth of the Royal Navy as many British sailors first gained experience on board slave ships.

Manufacturing

- Goods manufactured in Britain were used to buy enslaved Africans. These goods included textiles, metals such as iron, copper and brass, and metal goods such as pots, pans and cutlery.
- Cloth manufacturing grew, particularly in Manchester, due to supplies of slave-produced cotton.

Raw materials

- The slave trade was important in providing British industries with raw materials. The raw materials would be turned into manufactured goods in Britain and then sold for large profits in Europe.
- Liverpool grew wealthy from slave-grown cotton, while Bristol's wealth was partly based on slave-produced sugar.

Slaves cutting sugar cane

Industrial development

- Factories supplying goods to the slave traders developed.
- Banks and insurance companies which offered services to slave merchants expanded. London grew very wealthy as a result.
- Canals and railways were built as a result of investment of profits from the slave trade.
- Profits from the slave trade were invested in the development of industries.
- Some historians believe that the slave trade was central to Britain's industrial development. However, the slave trade was not always profitable. Changes in agriculture and advances in technology also contributed to Britain's wealth.

Wealth of ports and individuals

- Ports such as Bristol and Liverpool became wealthy trading centres due to their direct involvement in the trading of slaves. Liverpool became the main slave trading port.
- Other ports and cities profited from trading in goods connected with the slave trade.
- Huge fortunes were made by slave merchants who often bought large country estates or built large town houses. Some merchants used their wealth from the slave trade to invest in banks, industries or new businesses.
- Jobs such as shipbuilders, rope makers and dockworkers were created in British ports and many people gained employment in factories which supplied goods to the slave traders. Many British people owed their livelihood to the slave trade.

Glasgow Gallery of Modern Art was built in 1780 as the townhouse of the wealthy tobacco lord, William Cunninghame of Lainshaw.

> **TOP TIP**
>
> 'There is not a brick in the city but what is cemented with the blood of a slave.' Many buildings built for the slave trade can still be seen today.

Quick Test

1. Name the two main British slave trading ports.
2. Which tropical crop made the most profit for Britain?
3. How did the slave trade benefit the Royal Navy?
4. How did merchants spend their fortunes made from the slave trade?

The captive's experience and slave resistance

Humanitarian concerns

Although the treatment of captives in the slave factories, their conditions on slave ships and their treatment on the plantations were inhumane, there were some examples of slaves being treated with a degree of humanity:

- Some slaves were treated more humanely on smaller West Indian plantations.
- Some humane slave ship captains eased the harsh conditions of the Middle Passage.
- **Loose Pack**: Ships carried fewer slaves using this method, which meant slaves had more room and could lie down. The motives behind this method were more financial than humanitarian since a higher survival rate meant larger profits.
- In 1788 the British Parliament introduced Dolben's Law which controlled the number of slaves a slave ship could carry and required ships to have a doctor on board. The death rate among slaves was reduced as a result. Again, it is thought the motives were financial, in order to make bigger profits.
- Although slave traders claimed they gave opportunities for the slaves to exercise on board, the reality was that occasional exercise on deck was forced on the slaves. The slaves were whipped and the women were often abused.

TOP TIP

The logbooks of captains and surgeons on slave ships are valuable primary sources of the slave trade.

Religious concerns

Slave owners and traders used religion to justify their participation in the slave trade by referring to the existence of slavery in the Bible. Some even claimed slavery had a positive effect as it exposed Africans to Christianity. Gradually, some Christian groups began to turn against the slave trade:

- **Society of Friends or Quakers**: When the Society for the Abolition of the Slave Trade was formed in 1787, nine out of the twelve founding members were Quakers.
- **Methodists**: The Methodist leader, John Wesley, wrote *Thoughts on Slavery* in 1774 criticising the slave trade. Methodists also supported boycotts of slave produced goods.

Financial considerations

Financial concerns dominated the relationship between slaves and the slavers.

- Slaves were chosen for their ability to do manual work.
- Slaves were washed, shaved and rubbed with oil to make them look healthy before being sold at auction. Sick or 'refuse' slaves were often left to die.

- Slave ships carried as many slaves as possible (between 350–600 slaves) to make as much profit as possible. The method of **Tight Pack** involved carrying as many slaves as possible knowing that many would die but a large number would survive the voyage.
- Slaves who fell ill on the Middle Passage were often thrown overboard to prevent the spread of disease.
- Slaves were forced to work for long hours, particularly on the sugar plantations. Slaves were seen as property and were cheap enough to work, or beat, to death. This was known as 'wastage'.

Fear of revolt

- **Middle Passage**: Slaves were held in chains below deck, with little freedom for movement. Rebellions were dealt with harshly.
- **Plantations**: Floggings, stocks, chains and neck clamps were common punishments for acts of resistance. Draconian laws were passed in the West Indian islands to discourage runaways.

Slaves being burnt at the stake for being suspected of plotting revolt.

Racism and prejudice

The treatment of enslaved Africans was often justified by racism; there was a mistaken belief that Africans were inferior to Europeans.

- Slave traders often believed that African captives would otherwise be executed since many had committed crimes or had been prisoners of war.
- There was a lack of understanding about African culture. Plantation owners believed that slaves were fortunate to be given homes and employment.
- Slaves were treated not as fellow human beings but as property.

Quick Test

1. How did Dolben's Law in 1788 improve conditions on board slave ships?
2. Which two Christian groups spoke out against the slave trade?
3. What sometimes happened to sick slaves on board slave ships?
4. Why were harsh laws passed in the West Indian islands?

The abolitionist campaigns

The abolitionist movement

In 1787 the Society for the Abolition of the Slave Trade was formed in London. Its initial aim was to win over Members of Parliament to the abolitionist cause. **MP William Wilberforce** led the abolition campaign inside Parliament. He introduced bills to abolish the slave trade over a period of 18 years.

Arguments of the abolitionists

- Slave trade was un-Christian. It was immoral to use fellow human beings as slaves.
- Slave trade was inhumane. Slaves were denied their freedom and human rights.
- Slave trade was uneconomic. Britain's dependence on the slave trade hindered the development of domestic industries.

The abolitionists decided it was easier to campaign for the abolition of the slave trade than the abolition of slavery itself, since an important part of Britain's wealth depended on products produced by slaves and slave owners might demand compensation.

Abolitionist methods

Local and regional abolition committees were set up and organised meetings and activities including publishing pamphlets, posters and newspaper articles. Notable campaigners included:

- **Thomas Clarkson:** collected and publicised a wide range of evidence of the slave trade such as handcuffs, branding irons and thumbscrews; also, most importantly, the drawing of the Liverpool slave ship *The Brookes*.
- **Josiah Wedgwood:** china manufacturer who produced the society's slogan and design *'Am I Not A Man And A Brother?'* which appeared on cups, saucers and jewellery.
- **Olaudah Equiano:** gave first-hand evidence of his life as a slave. His book *An Interesting Life of Olaudah Equiano* was a best seller and changed many people's views of the slave trade.
- **John Newton:** provided a first-hand account by a slaver. A former slave trade ship's captain who changed his opinion on slavery and became a clergyman; an influential preacher and writer on the cruelty of the slave trade.

The drawing of the Liverpool slave ship The Brookes

Defenders of the trade

However, the slave trade had many important supporters.

- Plantation owners: the slave trade had made them very wealthy. Some bribed MPs to vote against abolition bills.
- There was a strong pro-slavery lobby within Parliament. Some MPs were also plantation owners or had businesses linked to the slave trade.
- The major ports of Liverpool and Bristol argued in favour of the slave trade.

The abolitionist campaign suffered a setback due to the French Revolution and Britain's war with France. The ideas of the abolitionists were regarded as being dangerous. It was much harder during this time for abolitionists to hold public meetings

The debate: why did the abolition campaign succeed?

In 1807 Parliament banned the slave trade. Why was the abolition campaign eventually successful?

- **Public opinion.** All levels of society were involved in the abolition campaign, reading abolitionist literature and attending meetings. Over 300 000 took part in the sugar boycott.
- **Pro-abolition MPs.** In 1792 the House of Commons voted in favour of the gradual abolition of the slave trade although the bill was rejected by the House of Lords. Through these MPs' perseverance, an abolition bill was finally passed in Parliament in February 1807.
- **British economy**. Some historians argue that Britain's industries no longer depended on the triangular trade.

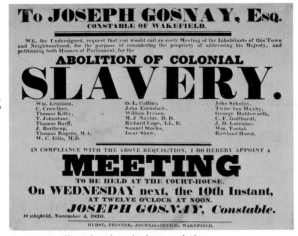

Petition calling for the abolition of Slavery

TOP TIP

Has too much importance been given to William Wilberforce? It is important to remember the other key abolitionists who contributed. Many ordinary men and women also played important roles in the abolitionist campaigns.

Quick Test

1. Why did the abolitionists decide to concentrate on abolishing the slave trade rather than slavery?
2. What was the name of the former African slave who wrote a best-selling book about his experiences as a slave?
3. Name three groups who defended the slave trade.
4. Give three reasons for the success of the abolitionist campaign in 1807.

Timeline

1772 – The Somerset Ruling. The law in England rules that a slave cannot be removed from Britain by force and sold into slavery.

1783 – The Zong trial. The captain of the Zong is taken to court on charges of fraud against his insurance company after 132 slaves were murdered by being thrown overboard in order to claim insurance.

1787 – The Society for the Abolition of the Slave Trade is formed.

1788 – The Dolben Act introduces controls on the number of slaves ships can carry.

1789 – The French Revolution (the revolutionaries opposed slavery). William Wilberforce introduces his first abolition bill which is defeated.

1791 – Over 300 000 people join the sugar boycott.

1792 – 519 petitions against the slave trade, signed by 390 000 people are presented to Parliament.

1793 – War with France. The abolition campaign suffers a decline in support.

1806 – Foreign Slave Trade Act passed.

1807 – Abolition of the Slave Trade Act. British Parliament bans the slave trade.

Biographies

Granville Sharp (1735–1813)

Granville Sharp was a civil servant and one of the founder members of the Society for the Abolition of the Slave Trade. He campaigned against the slave trade through the law courts. In 1772 he defended James Somerset and in 1783 he was involved in the court case against the captain of the Zong.

Hannah More (1745–1833)

Hannah More was a poet and author who supported the abolition of the slave trade. She helped organise the sugar boycott and encouraged other women to campaign against the slave trade.

James Stephen (1758–1832)

James Stephen joined the abolition movement after witnessing the treatment of slaves in the West Indies and played an influential role in the final stages of the abolition campaign. He used his background as a lawyer to draft a bill banning British subjects from participating in the slave trade with France and her allies. The bill passed and became the Foreign Slave Trade Act which brought an end to two-thirds of Britain's slave trade.

William Wilberforce (1759–1833)

William Wilberforce was an MP for Hull and then for Yorkshire. He was introduced to the Society for the Abolition of the Slave Trade by his friend John Newton. He became the Society's leader and led the abolition campaign in Parliament. He was an inspirational speaker and debater who, despite facing strong opposition from supporters of the slave trade, introduced abolition bills every year from 1789 to 1807 and gradually won over Parliament to end the slave trade.

William Pitt (1759–1806)

William Pitt was Prime Minister from 1783 to March 1804 and again from May 1804 to 1806. Pitt was a friend of William Wilberforce and a supporter of the abolition of the slave trade. However, the slave revolt in 1791 in St Domingue (Haiti) and the wars with France made it difficult for Pitt to continue supporting abolition.

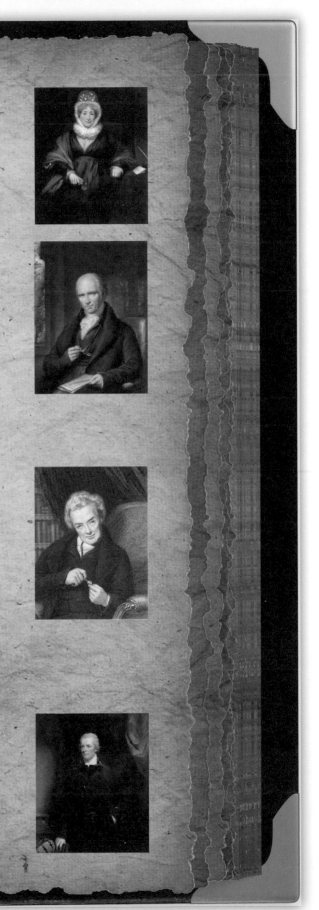

Health and housing

In eighteenth and nineteenth century Britain, life expectancy was much lower than it is now. This was due to two very closely linked factors: poor health and poor housing.

Why was the health of the urban population so bad?

DID YOU KNOW?

The cholera epidemics actually improved living conditions in the long term, because they affected all classes of society. When the middle and upper classes were infected, the government was forced to act.

Lack of sanitation	• Open sewers attracted rats and flies and disease. • Communal toilets meant disease spread more easily. • Sewage from midden heaps and cesspools polluted the water supply.
Dirty water supply	• A shortage of fresh clean water meant disease spread quickly.
Lack of hygiene	• Few washing facilities meant people could not keep clean. • Clothes were difficult to wash, so lice were common. • Soap was expensive.
Poor diet	• A lack of fresh food in towns meant shortages of vitamins and minerals. • Alcoholism was common as people drank beer or gin because both tasted better than dirty water!
Killer diseases	• There was no cure for many diseases. • Thousands died every year of diseases such as cholera, tuberculosis, scarlet fever, smallpox, typhus and typhoid.
Poor housing	• Overcrowding meant diseases spread more easily. • Because of the window tax, people blocked up windows. This led to poor ventilation and air-borne diseases, for example influenza and tuberculosis. The tax was only removed in 1851.
Lack of support from the state	• The government took a laissez-faire approach which meant no help for those in poverty that needed it.

Why did the situation improve?

Problem...	Tackled by...
Lack of sanitation	• **1848 Public Health Act** encouraged local councils to set up health boards to improve sanitation and water supply. • **1875 Public Health Act** forced local authorities to provide sewerage, drainage and clean water.
Dirty water supply	• Tackled by Health Acts above. • Reservoirs piped clean drinking water into cities.

Lack of hygiene	• The ending of the tax on soap/cheap carbolic soap meant people could wash properly.
	• Cotton clothes could be washed more easily and at higher temperatures.
Poor diet	• Improvements to farming meant there was a better food supply.
	• Better transport meant fresh meat, milk and vegetables could be bought in the cities.
	• Tea became a fashionable and healthy alternative to beer.
Killer diseases	• Greater medical knowledge and cleaner hospitals led to fewer deaths.
	• Better diet helped reduce deaths from tuberculosis.
	• Cholera and typhoid almost disappeared with cleaner water.
	• 1853 **Vaccination Act** made smallpox vaccination compulsory.
Poor housing	• **185**5 Nuisance Removal Act allowed councils to demolish the worst slum housing.
	• 1875 Artisans' and Labourers' Dwellings Improvement Act gave councils more power to demolish slums.
Lack of support from the state	• Still little help for the poorest families due to the laissez-faire attitude of government.

Why was the health of the rural population so bad?

- Working hours were very long – exhaustion left people open to illness.
- Houses were damp – this led to the spread of diseases like tuberculosis.
- Diet lacked variety and vitamins.
- Living with animals often led to further diseases – bovine tuberculosis was common.

However, the health of the rural population was not as bad as the health of the urban population. Why was this?

- Less overcrowding, so diseases did not spread as quickly.
- Sanitation facilities were not shared with as many people.
- Water supply tended to be cleaner.
- Although the diet was poor it was generally better than in the towns and cities, with more fresh food available.

Quick Test

1. What were the killer diseases of the nineteenth century?
2. Why was the window tax bad for public health?
3. Which acts improved poor housing in the nineteenth century?
4. Why was health and housing better in the countryside?

Factories and mines

Coal mining

- Adult males tended to be 'hewers' who cut the coal with hand tools.
- Women and older children tended to be 'bearers', who carried coal up the mine shaft, or 'drawers', who pulled the coal in carts along the bottom of the mine to the shaft.
- Small children were often 'trappers' who opened and closed trap doors.

An investigation into mine conditions in 1840 revealed just how terrible they were. This encouraged the government to intervene. New laws included:

- 1842: Children under 10 and all females banned from working in the mines.
- 1862: Single mine shafts declared illegal.
- 1872: Mine managers had to have certificates to prove that they were trained.

By 1900 mining was a safer job, but it was still hard, physical work in poor conditions.

Condition...	Tackled by...
Cutting coal	• In Scotland, the first coal cutting machinery ('Gartsherrie') used in 1864.
Poor ventilation: Lots of dust caused lung diseases like 'black spit'. It was also highly flammable.	• Two-shaft mines became more common. • Trap doors kept the air moving. • Ventilation fans installed from the 1860s onwards.
Transporting coal: Accidents occurred due to bearers falling and trappers being run over	• From 1844, steam engines pulled hutches on rails. • Wire rope used from about 1850. • Steam-powered winding engines.
Flooding: Common as mines became deeper and drilled into underground lakes and rivers.	• Steam-powered pumps.
Gas: Some gases were explosive and others suffocated miners.	• Davy Safety Lamp invented in 1815. • Ventilation fans.
Roof falls: Very common before 1850. Miners were crushed to death or died of starvation if trapped.	• Wooden pit props were replaced by hydraulic, metal pit props by 1900.

Conditions in factories

- **Poor ventilation:** Lots of dust caused tuberculosis and other diseases.
- **Dangerous machinery:** Machines were unfenced and had to be cleaned or repaired while they were still running. No safety laws to protect workers.
- **Long working hours:** Before 1833, 14-hour days were common. Workers rarely had more than a 30-minute break. Tiredness caused many accidents
- **Loud machinery:** The noise was literally deafening.
- **Hot, damp environment:** Factories were very humid in order to stop the cotton threads from breaking. This was very bad for the workers' health.
- **Risk of fire:** Due to the cotton fibres, explosions were common.

What was the impact of new technology?

- New machines like Arkwright's water frame and Crompton's mule sped up spinning and factories became more productive.
- Power looms increased the production of weaving.
- However, there was significant unemployment among hand spinners and weavers.
- New technology brought more accidents and more dust.
- Overall, the increased productivity meant that there were more jobs available.

Laws passed to improve conditions

1833 Factory Act	• No children under 9 allowed. • Maximum 8-hour working day for children aged 9–13. • Children were not allowed to clean machines while in motion.
1844 Factory Act	• Maximum 6½-hour working day for children under 13. • Maximum 12-hour working day for women and all under 18s. • Fencing of dangerous machinery became a legal requirement.
1847 Factory Act	• Maximum 10-hour working day for women and all under 18s.
1850 Factory Act	• Working day increased to 10½ hours.
1878 Factory Act	• No child under 10 was to be employed. • 10–14 year olds could only be employed for half days. • Women could work no more than 56 hours per week.

Despite these laws, by 1900 conditions in the factories were still dangerous and difficult.

Quick Test

1. What was 'black spit'?
2. Why was the Davey Safety Lamp important in improving miners' safety?
3. Why was repairing factory machinery so dangerous?
4. Name two pieces of technology that sped up factory work.

Canals and railways

Canals

Britain's first major canal opened in 1761. The Bridgewater Canal transported coal to the industrial centre of Manchester. This was very economical compared to the horse and cart.

By the 1770s the canal network was developing across the midlands of England. By 1830 there was over 4000 miles of canal connecting up many of the major industrial cities of Britain. Key rivers like the Thames were connected to the country towns and farms like never before. The Grand Junction Canal linked London with the rest of the country's canals. Coal, wood, food and people were all transported in growing numbers throughout the early nineteenth century.

How did canals develop in Britain?

The network of canals was built by inland navigators ('navvies') – often Irish immigrants. The canals had to be virtually flat, so great feats of engineering were required to build them (for example aqueducts).

From the end of the eighteenth century, locks came into common use. Locks enable canal boats to move from one level to another.

Why did canals go into decline?

Transport by canal was always going to be slow. It also depended on the destination being near a canal. Trains were cheaper, faster, less affected by the weather and could carry much more than canal boats.

Railways

The idea of putting a cart on a track was not new and wooden wagon ways had been used before. By the early nineteenth century, improvements in iron production meant that metal tracks could be made and the invention of the steam locomotive in 1808 meant heavier loads could be pulled.

In 1825 the first public railway was opened between Stockton and Darlington. By the end of the nineteenth century almost every town and city in Britain was linked by a network of 22 000 miles of rail track.

How were the railways built?

Most of the railways were built by men who used picks, shovels, spades and barrows to shift the earth. Navvies built viaducts, cut into the sides of hills, blasted tunnels and built embankments and bridges.

Improvements to rail travel
Safety
- By the 1840s there was mechanical signalling on the tracks. Block signalling was introduced in 1889.

- By 1889 trains had continuous braking systems which were enforced by the 1889 Regulation of Railways Act.

Comfort

- By the 1840s, third class carriages had seats and roofs. First and second class had toilets, heating and lighting from the 1870s.
- Journeys also became much quicker as the average speed rose. Building bridges also shortened journey times. The Tay Bridge and the Forth Bridge made travel in Scotland much quicker from the 1870s.

Forth Rail Bridge being built

DID YOU KNOW?

Britain experienced a period of 'railway mania' when it was really fashionable to travel by train. However, some people were concerned that travelling so fast would cause heart attacks and damage passengers' health permanently. Farmers worried that sparks from the trains would set fire to their crops and the noise would frighten their animals.

What was the impact of the railway networks?

	Positive	Negative
Economy	• Investors in railways made fortunes. • Many jobs created by the railways. • Coal and iron industries boomed. • Shopping trips and other holidays boosted the economy in tourist towns.	• Towns not connected by train went into decline. • Canals declined. • Turnpike roads and coaching inns lost business.
Society	• Diet improved as fresh food could be brought in from the farms. • People could commute to work, meaning they did not have to live close to factories. • Postal service was more efficient.	• Some farmers had their land 'invaded' by noisy, dirty trains. • Fatal accidents when building the railways were common. • The Tay Bridge disaster (1879) killed 75 people due to faulty bridge design.

Quick Test

1. Why was canal transport cheaper than horse and cart?
2. Why did canals go into decline?
3. What is a 'navvie'?
4. How did railways help improve urban health?

Democratic reform up to 1867

Radical protest

The right to vote is key in a democratic country.

In 1800 less than 3% of the population had the right to vote. People started to demand change and when this did not happen, some became more radical in their demands.

One such example was the so-called 'Peterloo Massacre' of 1819. On the 16 August, Henry Hunt was speaking to around 80 000 people in St Peter's Field, Manchester. Local yeomanry attacked the crowd, killing 15 unarmed protestors and injuring hundreds of others.

A second example, in the following year, was the 'Battle of Bonnymuir' (near Glasgow). People were angry at high prices, rising taxes and unemployment among handloom weavers and farm workers.

In February of 1820, 27 Radicals were arrested on suspicion of planning an uprising and urging people to commit treason. A strike in Glasgow was encouraged and some Radicals marched to Carrongrange to seize weapons. The Radicals and the government clashed at Bonnymuir. Four of the Radicals were injured and the rest were arrested.

Another group of Radicals marched from Strathaven to Glasgow, but were also stopped by government troops. Fifty of the Radicals were tried for treason and three were publicly executed. Nineteen others were deported to Australia.

Battle of Bonnymuir memorial

THINK POINT

Were the uprisings a real threat to the government? Think about the scale of the protest and the government's reaction.

What did the 1832 Great Reform Act do?

- Gave the vote to 1 in 5 men, mostly in the middle classes.
- Gave more seats to the new industrial towns.
- Abolished rotten boroughs.

However, 90% of the population could not vote; the unelected House of Lords was very powerful; only wealthy, property-owning males could become MPs and the voting system was riddled with bribery and corruption.

The Chartists

Who?	• A group of campaigners based in the north of England.	
How did they campaign?	• Held meetings. • Wrote letters and sent petitions to parliament. • Published leaflets and newspapers. • Organised strikes and marches. • Would resort to violent demonstration if necessary.	Universal male suffrage Secret ballot voting system Fairer distribution of seats/equal constituency size Payment of MPs (and the removal of property qualifications) Annual elections
Were they successful?	• They failed to gain support in parliament or with the middle classes. • They raised awareness of the demand for reform. • Their influence can be seen in the 1867 Reform Act.	*The People's Charter*

What did the 1867 Reform Act do?

For the first time, all male householders over 21 living in towns were given the vote. This meant some working class men were enfranchised for the first time and the electorate tripled.

There were still significant undemocratic features:

- No women could vote.
- Voting was public and open to bribery and corruption.
- Only wealthy people could become an MP.
- The House of Lords was very powerful.

Britain had some way to go to become a democracy.

Quick Test

1. How did the government deal with radical unrest?
2. Why were some people not satisfied with the 1832 Reform Act?
3. What did the Chartists want?
4. Why was the 1867 Reform Act seen as a step in the right direction?

Timeline

1761 – Bridgewater Canal opened.

1815 – The Davey Safety Lamp invented.

1819 – The 'Peterloo Massacre'.

1820 – The 'Battle of Bonnymuir'.

1825 – Stockton to Darlington railway opened.

1832 – The Great Reform Act passed.

1842 – Children under 10 banned from working in mines.

1851 – Window tax abolished.

1867 – The Second Reform Act passed.

1853 – Smallpox vaccinations made compulsory.

Biographies

Edward Jenner (1749–1823)

Jenner developed a vaccine against smallpox. He discovered that infecting people with the minor cowpox disease prevented them from getting smallpox. The word 'vaccine' comes from the Latin word *vacca* meaning cow. Smallpox was virtually wiped out in the 1970s and very few cases are diagnosed worldwide today.

Thomas Telford (1757–1834)

He was an engineer responsible for much of the transport infrastructure across Scotland and the rest of Britain. He designed and built canals, roads, harbours and tunnels. He built some of Britain's most impressive viaducts. Later in life he was known as the 'Colossus of Roads' due to his involvement with road building across Britain.

George Stephenson (1781–1848)

Stephenson was an engineer and inventor most famous for developing the 'Rocket' steam locomotive. The Rocket could travel at a record 36 miles per hour. Stephenson was responsible for building the Stockton to Darlington railway and designed the first passenger railway between Liverpool and Manchester.

Henry Hunt (1773–1835)

Henry Hunt was a radical speaker and huge influence on the Chartist movement. He was a superb public speaker and generated significant support for the radical movement for democracy. It was Henry Hunt who was speaking before the Peterloo massacre in 1819.

Benjamin Disraeli (1804–1881)

Disraeli was Conservative Prime Minister in the 1860s and 1870s. He played a key role as Chancellor of the Exchequer at the time of the 1867 Reform Act. He had significant rivalry with his Liberal counterpart, William Gladstone. Many credit Disraeli with creating a more modern Conservative Party. He also played a key role in Britain's involvement in the Suez Canal.

Divided society: poverty, housing, politics

In the late nineteenth and early twentieth centuries, there was little help available to the poor. It was commonly thought that poverty was caused by moral, personal or even genetic defects. Politicians believed in *laissez-faire*, that is, they thought it was not the responsibility of the government to interfere in people's private lives.

What help was available to the poor?

The Poor Law

The Poor Law, passed in 1834, created work houses (or poor houses in Scotland) to provide help for the needy. The conditions were deliberately harsh so that it would be a last resort. Families were split up, inmates were forced to wear a uniform and the diet was poor. One Victorian writer referred to poor houses as 'prisons for the poor'. They were feared and hated, so only about 10% of people who needed relief actually received it.

Dinner time at St Pancras Workhouse in London, circa 1911

Self help

In 1850 a Scotsman called Samuel Smiles wrote the book *Self-Help*. Smiles wrote that the best way to get out of poverty was through hard work and effort. He wrote 'God helps those who help themselves.' Unfortunately, Smiles failed to recognise that poverty was often caused by factors outwith an individual's control. Smiles' book reinforced the idea that if you were poor it was your own fault.

Charity

Many charitable organisations were formed at the turn of the century to help the poor. The Salvation Army, Dr Barnado's and the YMCA were all formed during this period. While they did help the poor, they were unco-ordinated and many poor received no effective help.

Slum housing in Glasgow, 1861

Why did attitudes towards poverty change?

Investigations into poverty

Towards the end of the nineteenth century, several writers studied the lives of the poor. Charles Booth wrote *Life and Labour of the People in London* between 1886 and 1903 and Seebohm Rowntree wrote *Poverty: A Study of Town Life* in 1901 about the city of York.

What did the investigations discover?

- Rowntree calculated that £1·08 a week was the minimum income to keep a family above the 'poverty line'. Anyone living below this was deemed to be in poverty.
- According to their calculations 30% of the population were living below the poverty line.
- They identified the causes of poverty as sickness, old age, unemployment, low wages and large families rather than laziness and moral failings as had been previously thought.

The reports were influential because they used statistical data that proved that poverty was a major problem in Britain.

Emergence of the Labour Party

The emergence of the Labour Party after 1900 gave the working class a party to represent their interests. Both the Liberals and the Conservatives had to compete with Labour for working class votes, so were forced to take the issue of poverty seriously.

National security

The Boer War of 1889–1902 revealed that almost 25% of volunteers for the army were rejected on grounds of ill health. This figure was even higher in cities. The government was concerned that Britain could not protect its Empire or win a war if its young men were not fit enough to fight because of childhood poverty.

Genuine concern

A new generation of politicians were genuinely concerned about poverty. The Liberal Leader David Lloyd George had been brought up in a poor family in Wales.

Quick Test

1. What does *'laissez-faire'* mean?
2. Why was the help available to the poor ineffective?
3. What was the poverty line?
4. What did investigations of Booth and Rowntree reveal as the main causes of poverty?

Liberal Reforms 1906–1914

The reforms

Between 1906 and 1914 the Liberal government introduced a series of social reforms to improve the lives of the poor. Five main groups in society were targeted.

The young

There was genuine concern that Britain would lose its position as a global power in the future due to the poor health of children. Three reforms were passed.

- **Education (Provision of Meals) Act 1906**
  - Local councils could raise taxes to **pay f**or free school meals for children.
  - It was not compulsory, however, so many councils did nothing and the problem was not solved.

- **Education (Administrative Provisions) Act 1907**
  - Every child would receive three free medical inspections during their school career.
  - This was successful in identifying chronic health problems, but did nothing to treat them.

- **Children's Charter 1908**
  - Children were banned from begging, smoking and drinking alcohol.
  - Special children's courts and prisons were introduced to keep juveniles away from adult criminals.

Children drinking and smoking, circa 1905

The old

David Lloyd George famously said that the elderly who had worked all of their lives should not be allowed to reach 'the gates of the tomb … through the brambles and thorns of poverty'.

- **Old Age Pensions Act 1908**
  - Entitled people over 70 who earned between £21 and £31 a year to a maximum weekly pension of 25 pence.
  - This was 10 pence less than the amount needed to stay above the poverty line.
  - Life expectancy for the working poor was much less than 70 so most people died before receiving a pension.

The sick

The poor often struggled to pay for medical treatment. There was no free healthcare so illness often went untreated, leading to absence from work.

- **National Insurance Act (Part 1) 1911**
  - A contributory scheme in which the worker paid 4 pence, the employer 3 pence and the government 2 pence a week.
  - If a worker was absent through ill health they would receive benefits for 26 weeks.
  - Critics argue that the contributions to the scheme from workers' wages meant they were paid less, so actually made poverty worse.

The unemployed

Reforms were introduced to help those out of work.

- **Labour exchanges**
  - The government introduced labour exchanges where workers could register their skills and employers would advertise their vacancies. By 1914 3000 people were finding employment every day.
  - Critics argue that the exchanges only helped people find other low paid and temporary work, so did not improve poverty.
- **National Insurance Act (Part 2) 1911**
  - A contributory scheme that covered workers in specific heavy industries if they became unemployed.
  - It was limited because it only covered around two million workers.
  - Contributions from wages made poverty worse.

The employed

The Liberals also introduced a series of reforms to tackle the issue of low pay and poor working conditions, for example:

- The Coal Mines Act (1908) introduced an 8-hour working day for miners.
- The Minimum Wage Act (1912) set up a minimum wage for miners.

How successful were the Liberal reforms?

Some argue that while the reforms did go some way to easing the problems of poverty, they did not solve them. Many people were still living below the poverty line defined by Rowntree.

However, others argue that the Liberal reforms were crucial in ending the *'laissez-faire'* attitude towards poverty. For the first time ever the government introduced laws to improve the living standards of the people. The reforms have been described as 'the greatest ever passed by one government up to that time'.

> **THINK POINT**
>
> The turn of the century was a very unsettled time in Britain. The campaign for women's suffrage, European conflict in the build-up to the First World War and political problems in Ireland were all major problems for the government. Given this context, should the Liberal reforms be considered a success or a failure?

Quick Test

1. Which five groups did the Liberals focus their reforms upon?
2. Why were the Liberals concerned about the health of children?
3. Why can it be argued that some of the reforms actually made the problems of poverty worse?
4. Why can it be argued that the reforms were successful, even though they did not eradicate poverty?

Social impact of the Second World War in Britain

The interwar years

Despite the best efforts of the Liberal government between 1906 and 1914, there was still a significant problem of poverty in Britain between the First and Second World Wars. These problems were made worse by a global depression triggered by the Wall Street Crash, declining industry and high levels of unemployment. The outbreak of the Second World War and the formation of the wartime coalition government brought the issue of poverty into the limelight once more.

The effects of the Second World War on attitudes to poverty

Bombing

The German Air Force targeted big industrial cities in Britain. Both rich and poor were affected. Over 61 000 civilians lost their lives and over four million homes were damaged or destroyed. Even Buckingham Palace was bombed. Wealthy people were now forced to rely on government help and rich and poor found themselves shoulder to shoulder in air raid shelters. Support increased for government intervention into social problems.

Effects of bombing in Aberdeen

Rationing

Rationing was introduced to ensure that there was a fair distribution of food and fuel for all people. Rich and poor were equally affected and this equality of sacrifice brought about a change in social attitudes.

Evacuation

Children from inner city areas were evacuated to rural areas to protect them from bombing raids. People in the country were often horrified at the poverty they witnessed among the children they homed. They gained a much better understanding of the problems of urban poverty and demanded something was done.

The Beveridge Report and the Five Giants

In 1942 the coalition government asked Sir William Beveridge to produce a report to show how a welfare state could be created. Sir William Beveridge had been a key adviser to the Liberals when they passed their social reforms between 1906 and 1914. A welfare state is one which looks after its people 'from the cradle to the grave', i.e. from birth to death.

He identified major problems, which he called 'the Five Giants' of poverty. He argued that all five needed to be eradicated if Britain was to lift all of its citizens out of poverty and hardship.

These were:

- **Want** – A lack of money
- **Disease** – Illness and poor health
- **Squalor** – Poor quality housing
- **Ignorance** – Lack of education
- **Idleness** – Unemployment

In order to tackle these giants Beveridge recommended a social security system that would be:

Comprehensive	It would cover all problems relating to poverty, from birth to death.
Universal	It would be available to everyone.
Contributory	People would make weekly payments to the scheme through their wages.
Non means tested	Benefits would be available to all, regardless of ability to pay.
Compulsory	All workers would have to contribute.

Inter-war reforms

It is important to realise that not all social reforms of this time were passed by the post-war Labour government. The 1944 Education Act for example was passed during the wartime coalition government by the Tory MP R.A. Butler. It set a minimum leaving age which meant that all pupils had to stay at school until the age of 15.

DID YOU KNOW?

Before the Beveridge Report and his recommendations to improve the health of the nation, a common present when someone reached 21 was to pay to have all of their teeth removed and false ones put in their place. This was because dental hygiene was so bad!

Quick Test

1. How did the Second World War change attitudes to poverty?
2. What is a welfare state?
3. What were the 'Five Giants' of poverty?
4. In order to effectively tackle the giants of poverty, what did Beveridge recommend a social security system should be?

Labour reforms – the welfare state, 1945–1951

At the end of the Second World War Labour won a landslide election and the new Prime Minister, Clement Attlee, planned to create a welfare state which would tackle all 'Five Giants'.

- **Want** – A lack of money
- **Disease** – Illness and poor health
- **Squalor** – Poor quality housing
- **Ignorance** – Lack of education
- **Idleness** – Unemployment

1945 Labour election poster

Social security

To tackle Want, the Labour government passed three acts;

- **National Insurance (Industrial Injuries) Act 1946**
  In return for weekly contributions, the government would provide benefits for anyone injured in the workplace who could not consequently earn a wage.

- **National Insurance Act 1946**
  A contributory scheme which entitled workers to unemployment, sickness, maternity and widows' benefits, a retirement pension and a funeral grant. The aim was to provide insurance 'from the cradle to the grave'.

- **National Assistance Act 1948**
  The previous reforms were only for people in work, but the government wanted to create a 'safety net' for those who could not afford to contribute to National Insurance. People could apply for further benefits if National Insurance did not cover their needs.

Criticisms of National Insurance

- Due to rising prices and wages after the war, welfare benefits in 1948 were only 19% of the average wage, not enough to lift people out of poverty.
- Too many people were therefore forced to apply for national assistance.

Health

To tackle Disease, Labour created the National Health Service (NHS), in 1948. It was set up with three main principles: it should be universal, comprehensive and free at the point of use. This meant it would be available to everybody, would cover any medical problem and would be funded by taxation, not by charges for treatment.

In the first year of the NHS millions benefited from free glasses, prescriptions and dental care. The biggest criticism was its cost. By 1950 the NHS was costing £358 million a year and taxes only paid for a fifth of this. In 1951 the government was forced to abandon the principle of 'free at the point of use' and introduce charges for false teeth and glasses.

Despite this, the NHS has been described as 'the single greatest achievement of the welfare state'.

> **TOP TIP**
>
> You should make a timeline of all the social reforms you have learned about in this topic. Colour code the timeline to show which reforms were passed by the Liberals, which by the wartime coalition government and which by Labour. This will help you to understand the chronology of social reform in Britain.

Housing reform

Overcrowding and slums had been a problem before the war and this was worsened by the destruction of approximately 700 000 homes in bombing raids.

Despite a shortage of building materials and labour force, the government built 200 000 homes a year between 1945 and 1951. Even this was not adequate, however, as the post-war baby boom years saw a rapid increase in population and demand for housing. A 1951 census showed that there were 750 000 fewer houses than were required.

Was the Labour government successful in creating a welfare state?

Some historians have criticised the reforms, arguing that poverty was not eradicated as outlined by William Beveridge.

Others have a much more positive view of the Labour government's achievements. Given that Britain was nearly bankrupted by the Second World War, they argue that Labour introduced a set of long lasting reforms which promoted a fair society. While poverty was not eradicated, help was provided to those in need and the general living standard of the poor was raised.

Quick Test

1. Which acts did Labour pass to solve the problem of Want?
2. Why can it be argued that Labour's social security reforms were ineffective?
3. What was the biggest criticism of the NHS?
4. Why did demand for housing grow after the war?

Timeline

1886 – Seebohm Rowntree begins investigating urban poverty in London.

1900 – Formation of the Labour Party.

1906 – The Liberals win a landslide election victory and begin introducing social reforms to improve the lives of the poor.

1914 – Outbreak of the First World War.

1929 – The Wall Street Crash in America triggers a global depression which leads to a decline in British industry and increased unemployment.

1939 – Outbreak of the Second World War leads to the suspension of party politics and the creation of the wartime coalition government.

1942 – The Beveridge Report is published.

1945 – Elections held at the end of the war lead to a landslide victory for the Labour Party.

1948 – The creation of the NHS.

Biographies

Charles Booth (1840–1916)

Booth was born into a wealthy family of shipbuilders and merchants in Liverpool. He was sceptical about a claim made by a politician that 25% of the population of London lived in poverty and so decided to investigate. He discovered that the figure was actually closer to 35%. His investigations, based on statistical data, proved to be very influential among politicians.

Seebohm Rowntree (1871–1954)

Born into the wealthy sweet manufacturing family, Rowntree was influenced by Booth and decided to investigate poverty in York. He discovered that almost 30% of the population were living in poverty. He defined the 'poverty line', stating the minimum amount of money needed to afford the basic necessities of life.

David Lloyd George (1863–1945)

Lloyd George was Chancellor at the time of the Liberal Reforms. He was responsible for the 'People's Budget' of 1909 which increased taxes on land to pay for welfare reforms. He was instrumental in setting up old age pensions and also in introducing sickness benefits.

William Beveridge (1879–1963)

Beveridge was a social reformer who advised the Liberal government on their welfare reforms. The wartime coalition government during the Second World War asked him to write a report recommending how a welfare state could be created. His report identified the 'Five Giants' of poverty and was widely supported by the British people.

Clement Attlee (1883–1967)

Attlee was the leader of the Labour Party during the Second World War and acted as the Deputy Prime Minister to Winston Churchill in the wartime coalition government. In 1945 he campaigned in elections by promising to implement the recommendations of the Beveridge Report. His party won a landslide victory and he set about introducing welfare reforms.

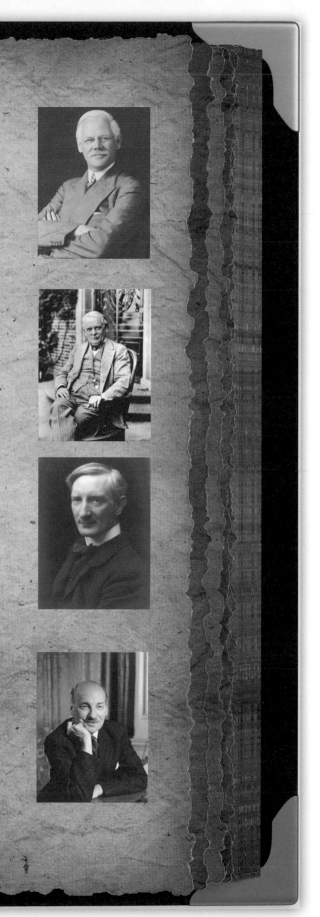

Imperial Russia – government and people

In 1894 Nicholas Romanov II became Tsar of Russia. He was a weak and poor leader, more interested in spending time with his family than ruling the country. Russia was an autocracy, which meant that the Tsar had absolute power over his subjects. Despite this, Russia was a very difficult country to govern.

Why was Russia difficult to govern?

Size
- The Russian Empire was huge. It contained approximately one seventh of all of the land on Earth.

DID YOU KNOW?

The only way to get from the west to the east of Russia was via the Trans-Siberian railway. This took a week!

Environment
- Russia was a cold, inhospitable place to live.
- Only a small part of the land was suitable for farming; most of the land was made up of frozen tundra, dense forest and desert.

People
- The Russian Empire contained over 130 million people, but less than half were ethnically Russian.
- Many people could not speak the Russian language and belonged to religions other than the official Orthodox Russian Church.
- The Tsarist government introduced the policy of Russification. Ethnic groups were banned from speaking their local language and were forced to learn Russian. They felt that their different ways of life were under attack.

Russian society

Peasants
- In 1914 peasants made up 85% of the population. The vast majority of these were poor, uneducated and illiterate. Their life expectancy was less than 40 years.
- Agricultural methods were backward and inefficient. Their way of farming (strip farming) was back breaking and led to low yields. They had little modern technology and used hand-made tools to work the land.

Workers
- In the cities poor industrial workers endured terrible conditions.
- Heavy industries such as steel, coal and iron were growing fast. Despite this, wages remained low and conditions were very poor. Accidents in the work place led to many deaths.

- Workers were forced to work overtime, sometimes up to 16 hours a day. They lived in overcrowded barracks provided by factory owners. These lacked basic sanitation.
- Occasionally workers would strike, but they were defeated by violence and bloodshed.

Middle class

- The Russian middle class grew at the start of the twentieth century due to the growth of business and industry. They were mainly wealthy and supportive of the Tsar as they owed their wealth to the government.

Nobles

- The super wealthy aristocracy owned over a quarter of the land, despite making up less than 1% of the population. They owned fabulous palaces, wore ostentatious fashions and dined at expensive restaurants.

Russian noblewoman, circa 1895

How did the Tsar rule Russia?

The Tsar was an autocrat, that is he had ultimate authority in government. He could not rule such a vast country on his own, however, so there was a system of government to help keep control.

Church	• The Church taught the Russian people that the Tsar was the 'Little Father', a living God.
Ministers	• The Tsar appointed ministers to run the government. They reported to him and he made the final decisions. He had the power to dismiss them whenever he saw fit.
Okhrana	• A secret police force whose function was to spy on potential enemies. • Suspected dissidents could be tortured, executed or exiled to the frozen wastes of Siberia.
Cossacks	• The Cossacks were violent horse-backed warriors who were used to put down any strikes or protests against the Tsar.

Quick Test

1. What does autocracy mean?
2. What was the policy of Russification?
3. What problems did the workers and peasants face in Tsarist Russia?
4. How did the Tsar keep control of Russia?

1905 Revolution – causes and events

Opposition to the Tsar

Several groups were prepared to oppose the Tsar.

- **Kadets** or **Liberals**: Middle class professionals who supported the Tsar but opposed autocracy. They wanted a democracy in which the Tsar would share power with a freely elected Parliament.
- **Socialist Revolutionaries:** Also known as the Peasants' Party, believed that all land should be confiscated and given to the peasants. They wanted to overthrow the Tsar.
- **Socialist Democrats**: Followed the teachings of Karl Marx; aimed to overthrow the Tsar and create a socialist state in which all land and wealth would be shared equally.

In 1903 the Socialist Democrats split into two groups: Bolsheviks and Mensheviks.

Bolsheviks	Mensheviks
• Led by Lenin. • Wanted a workers' revolution with no middle class involvement. • Believed revolution should be led by trained 'professional revolutionaries'. • Prepared to use violence if necessary.	• Led by Julius Martov. • Wanted a workers' revolution but with the help of the middle class. • Did not believe in use of violence.

TOP TIP

In order to fully understand the political ideas of the Bolsheviks, you should research the beliefs of Karl Marx as set out in 'The Communist Manifesto'.

The 1905 Revolution

In 1905 resentment among the workers and peasants grew and protests against the Tsar's government began.

What caused the 1905 Revolution?

- **Economic problems**: Peasants were taxed heavily to pay for improvements in industry. Poor harvests led to starvation.
- **The Russo-Japanese War:** Russia and Japan went to war over Manchuria. Russia's defeat led to protests about the incompetence of the Tsar.
- **Bloody Sunday:** In January 1905 a priest, Father Gapon, organised a peaceful march of 200 000 on the Winter Palace. The Tsar ordered the Cossacks to attack and a massacre occurred.

1905 Revolution: key events

- Landowners' homes were burned and looted.
- The Tsar's uncle was assassinated.
- The middle classes joined the protests.
- Sailors in the war rebelled against the Tsar.

- In September the Tsar signed a peace treaty with Japan.
- In October a general strike spread throughout major industrial cities.
- In December the Tsar used troops returning from the war to stop demonstrations.
- The revolution ended and the Tsar survived.

Fire in Odessa after the mutiny aboard the Potemkin battleship

What changed after 1905?

In October 1905 the Tsar signed the October Manifesto. He promised:
- A Duma (Parliament) elected by the people
- Civil rights
- Uncensored newspapers and the right to form political parties.

However, the Tsar did not give in to demands for greater democracy. The Duma had very little power and was inherently weak because the Tsar could dissolve it whenever he liked. While free speech had been guaranteed in 1905, censorship of newspapers continued.

Stolypin's reforms

In order to regain control the Tsar appointed a new Prime Minister, Peter Stolypin. He was known for his brutal punishment of revolutionaries, but he also introduced reforms to tackle some of the problems of poverty.

Countryside	Peasants were encouraged to buy land to create larger fields, yielding greater harvests. While production of food did increase slightly, there was not enough land to go round and farming methods remained backward.
Cities	Stolypin wanted to improve Russian industry. From 1906–14 there was an industrial boom in Russia. However, very few improvements were made to working and living conditions and as more workers moved into the cities, living conditions actually worsened.

Quick Test

1. Which groups opposed the Tsar?
2. What were the main causes of the 1905 Revolution?
3. Why was the Duma weak?
4. Who was appointed Prime Minister after 1905 and what did he do?

February Revolution – causes, events and effects

Causes of the 1917 February Revolution

War at the Front
- The Russian army suffered terrible casualties in the First World War. By the end of 1917 **1 300 000** soldiers had been killed, **4 200 000** had been wounded and **2 417, 000** taken prisoner.
- Russian soldiers blamed the Tsarist regime for the military defeats.

War at home
- The war caused huge economic problems for ordinary Russians.
- Agricultural output fell as millions of peasants and farm workers were conscripted into the army.
- Almost all of the trains were commandeered to take supplies to the front. This caused food and fuel shortages in the cities.
- Food and fuel prices increased but wages decreased. This led to strikes.

Influence of Rasputin
- The Tsar's son and heir, Alexis, suffered from the blood disease haemophilia. This was kept secret from the people.
- In desperation the Tsar sought help from a holy man called Rasputin. He was a coarse and drunken peasant, but was rumoured to have healing powers.
- He became part of the Tsar's entourage and eventually one of his most trusted advisers. He even influenced government decisions.
- The nobles were outraged and questioned the Tsar's judgement.

Unpopularity of the Tsarina
- In 1915 the Tsar went to the front to take command of the army. He left his German wife Alexandra to run the government.
- Rumours spread that Alexandra was a German spy.
- She was rumoured to be having an affair with Rasputin. This is probably untrue, but it increased the unpopularity of the royal family.

The Tsarina and her son, Alexis

The events of the February Revolution

- On 14 February 40 000 workers from the Putilov engineering works went on strike demanding higher wages and an end to food and fuel shortages.

- On International Women's Day (19 February) and the days that followed, over 200 000 workers took to the streets of Petrograd demanding cheaper food, higher wages and a new government.

- 27 February was the turning point. The Petrograd Garrison, which had been ordered to fire upon the protestors, mutinied and joined the revolution.

- The Tsar tried to return to Petrograd by train but was stopped by revolutionary rail workers.

- On 2 March the Tsar abdicated.

The February Revolution

The aftermath of the February Revolution

The abdication left a power vacuum which was filled by an alliance between the Provisional Government and the Petrograd Soviet, known as **Dual Power.**

- **Provisional Government:** Made up of ex-members of the Duma. They decided that they did not have the authority to make major decisions because they were not democratically elected. This was a fatal weakness. Russia needed strong leadership, but the Provisional Government did not provide it.

- **Petrograd Soviet:** A council of soldiers and sailors. They issued 'Order Number One', a proclamation which effectively gave them control of the army, railways and postal services. The Minister of War wrote: 'the Provisional Government exists only while this is permitted by the Soviet.'

In the early months of Dual Power, the Provisional Government did introduce some reforms, mainly aimed at increasing civil rights. These reforms did little to solve the main problems facing Russia: the continuing disaster of the war, the food and fuel shortages in the cities and the issue of land reform.

THINK POINT

It is sometimes said that the Provisional Government was doomed to failure from the start. Do you agree with this statement? What evidence would you use to explain your answer?

Quick Test

1. Why was the First World War so unpopular in Russia?
2. How did Rasputin damage the reputation of the Royal Family?
3. Why was the Petrograd Soviet more powerful than the Provisional Government?
4. Why did the Provisional Government fail to provide strong leadership?

October Revolution – causes, events, effects

The October Revolution

Events leading to the October Revolution

- **March 1917:** Lenin returned from exile in Switzerland and immediately argued for a second revolution. He issued a document known as the **'April Theses'**. This was simplified into two slogans; **'Peace, bread and land'** and **'All power to the Soviets'.** Bolsheviks were the only party to promise an end to the war.

- **July 1917 (July Days):** Bolsheviks attempted to lead a second revolution against the Provisional Government. They were defeated and Lenin fled to Finland.

- **August 1917:** General Kornilov threatened to invade Petrograd. The leader of the Provisional Government, Aleksandr Kerensky, asked the Bolshevik Red Guard to protect the city. They were given machine guns and rifles.

- Although Kornilov never reached Petrograd, the Bolsheviks were seen as saviours and kept their weapons. Kerensky and the Provisional Government looked weak and incompetent.

Lenin was convinced that conditions were perfect for a second revolution. He returned from exile in Finland and convinced the other Bolsheviks, who eventually agreed. Trotsky was put in charge of planning the revolution.

> **TOP TIP**
>
> When the Bolsheviks took power in October 1917 they changed the Russian calendar to make it match the western world. Because of this you will sometimes see the February Revolution referred to as the March Revolution and the October Revolution as the November Revolution.

Key events of the October Revolution

- On 24 October the Bolshevik Red Guards occupied railway stations, telephone exchanges, power stations and took control of the bridges over Petrograd's many canals and rivers.

- On 25 October Red Guards surrounded the Winter Palace which contained the remnants of the Provisional Government. At 9pm the battleship Aurora, crewed by revolutionary sailors, opened fire on the Winter Palace. The defenders of the palace fled and a small group of Bolsheviks entered and confronted the Provisional Government, who officially surrendered.

- Bolsheviks took control of Petrograd.

The Soviets in power

- In December 1917 Lenin set up the Chekha to suppress opponents of the Bolsheviks. Tens of thousands of civilians were executed without trial between 1918 and 1921 – this became known as the Red Terror.

- In March 1918 Lenin withdrew Russia from the War (Treaty of Brest-Litovsk).

Why did the Reds win the Civil War, 1918–21?

The Reds (Bolsheviks)	The Whites (Anti-Bolsheviks)
• Controlled the industrialised areas and most of the railways; could transport soldiers and supplies quickly.	• Were scattered around Russia and found it difficult to communicate or transport troops.
• An effective and disciplined fighting force.	• Unco-ordinated and ill disciplined.
• Depicted themselves as patriots fighting in defence of Russia; claimed the Whites were controlled by foreign enemies.	• Had help from Britain, France and the USA. However, they did not send enough troops or supplies to make a difference.
• Were well fed and supplied. Lenin introduced 'War Communism'. He requisitioned grain from peasants and took control of factories.	• Were poorly supplied.

Nature of the Soviet state

The economy

War communism caused a mass famine which killed 5 million people. Lenin was therefore forced to introduce the New Economic Policy (NEP) which:

- Stopped grain requisitioning.
- Maintained state control over major industries such as coal, oil, steel and railways. Smaller industries were allowed to be run under private ownership.
- Introduced a new currency and allowed the buying and selling of goods.
- Successfully ended famine in the countryside.

Despite this many Bolsheviks saw it as a betrayal of communist ideology.

Other changes

The Communists improved standards of literacy, increased women's rights and invested in the arts. However, poverty had barely improved; the people had endured a crippling famine, they lived in fear of the Chekha and they still could not vote.

Quick Test

1. Why was Lenin's return to Russia in March 1917 significant?
2. How did the Kornilov revolt help the Bolsheviks?
3. What promise did Lenin keep when the Bolsheviks took power?
4. Why was Trotsky an important figure for the Bolsheviks?

Timeline

1894 – Tsar Nicholas II becomes Tsar of Russia.

1905 – Russia breaks out in open revolt against the Tsar.

December 1905 – The Tsar regains control of Russia by deploying troops returning from the Russo-Japanese War.

1914 – Russia joins the war on the side of the Triple Entente.

1915 – The Tsar takes control of the Russian army, leaving the Tsarina in charge of the government.

February 1917 – Russia breaks out in revolution, the Tsar abdicates and the Provisional Government and the Petrograd Soviet rule with Dual Power.

October 1917 – The Bolsheviks lead a revolution against the Provisional Government, who eventually surrender and leave the Bolsheviks in charge.

March 1918 – Lenin signs the Treaty of Brest-Litovsk and pulls Russia out of the First World War.

1918–1921 – Russia erupts into Civil War between the Bolshevik Reds and the anti-Bolshevik Whites. In 1921 the Reds win.

Biographies

Tsar Nicholas Romanov II (1868–1918)

A member of the Romanov royal family, Nicholas ruled Russia from 1894 until 1917. He did little to solve the social problems in Russia and so peasants and workers became increasingly dissatisfied with his leadership. He survived an attempted revolution in 1905, but was forced to abdicate after the February Revolution in 1917.

Grigory Rasputin (1869–1916)

Rasputin was a peasant holy man who was rumoured to have supernatural healing powers. He was very unpopular among the Russian nobility because he was seen as a coarse and drunken peasant. His relationship with the Tsar was a contributing factor to the outbreak of the February Revolution.

Aleksandr Kerensky (1881–1970)

Kerensky was an important political figure after the February Revolution as he was the only man who was a member of the Provisional Government and the Petrograd Soviet. He was the Minister for War during the July Days and later became Prime Minister.

Lenin (1870–1924)

Lenin was the leader of the Bolsheviks and a professional revolutionary. He was in exile during the February Revolution, but immediately called for a second revolution on his return. After the October Revolution he became the leader of Russia. He ruled as a dictator and his policies were crucial in keeping the Red Army supplied during the Civil War.

Leon Trotsky (1879–1940)

Trotsky was Lenin's number two in the Bolsheviks. He was elected as Chairman of the Petrograd Soviet prior to the October Revolution. He planned the revolution in minute detail and was also in charge of the Red Army during the Civil War. He ensured discipline and made sure that the Red Army was an effective fighting force.

Weimar Germany

What happened at the end of World War I?

- German sailors mutinied at Kiel and Wilhelmshaven naval bases. The British blockade of Germany's ports meant food was not getting through and Germans were starving. The allies refused to sign a cease-fire unless the Kaiser abdicated.
- The Kaiser abdicated on 10 November 1918. The next day the cease-fire was signed and the First World War ended with Germany's defeat.
- The Weimar Republic was formed.

The Treaty of Versailles
There was widespread hatred among Germans of the terms of the Treaty of Versailles.

Term	Impact
Diktat	Resented being forced to sign the Treaty without negotiation.
War Guilt Clause	Hated being blamed for something that was not solely their fault.
Reparations of £6600 million.	Starvation continued after the war; loss of industrial land hindered recovery.
Severe reductions to army and navy. No air force allowed.	Humiliating, left Germany vulnerable to attack. Anger that no other country was treated similarly.
Excluded from League of Nations.	Insulted, isolated from future negotiations.

As a result, Germans called those who signed the Treaty 'November criminals'. These politicians formed the new Weimar government.

The Weimar government

A new government was formed in Weimar with a set of rules called a constitution. The first President was Friedrich Ebert. The constitution created the Reich (state) as a democratic country with a Chancellor and the Reichstag (parliament). Elections took place every four years and every German over the age of 20 could vote.

A President (voted for every seven years) had the power to prevent laws from being passed and they could close the parliament in the event of a 'national emergency' (Article 48).

What were the problems for the new Weimar government?
- Association with signing the very unpopular Treaty of Versailles.
- Rebuilding Germany after the war was difficult.
- Many wanted the return of a monarchy.
- Some thought the new republic was too left wing.

There were several attempts to overthrow the Weimar government. There was a left-wing revolt in 1919 (Spartacist Revolt) and two right-wing revolts: the Kapp Putsch in 1920 and the Munich Putsch in 1923.

TOP TIP
Putsch = German word for uprising
Mutiny = A revolt by soldiers or sailors
Abdicate = When a monarch gives up the throne
Reichstag = German parliament

Munich Beerhall Putsch

When?	November 1923
Where?	Munich, Bavaria
Who?	Right-wing/Nazi group led by Hitler
Why?	To overthrow the government and start a Nationalist revolution.
What?	• 600 armed followers stormed a meeting of Bavarian politicians. Hitler forced those politicians to support him.
	• 3000 Nazis marched the next day and were met with armed police. 14 Nazis were killed and Hitler was arrested.
	• Hitler was put on trial for treason and sent to Landsberg Castle jail.
	• The trial gave Hitler publicity and he became nationally known.

Economic crises

In response to the crisis in the Ruhr and other economic problems, the Weimar government decided to print more money in order to keep paying wages. Businesses put up prices. This resulted in *hyperinflation* – prices rose faster than people could spend the money.

163	250	463	1465	3465	69 000	1 512 000	1 743 000 000	201 000 000 000
Dec 1922	Jan 1923	Mar 1923	June 1923	July 1923	Aug 1923	Sept 1923	Oct 1923	Nov 1923

Price of bread (in marks), 1922–1923

Effects of hyperinflation: People were paid by the hour so they could spend the money before it became worthless, bartering became common, pensions became worthless, the poor became even poorer, the rich, land owners and anyone with large debts thrived.

After the Wall Street Crash of 1929, all Germans suffered economic problems. Businesses failed, wages decreased by an average of 60% and some industrial areas had an unemployment rate of over 50%.

How did the Great Depression weaken the Weimar government?
• The government became unpopular as it responded by raising taxes, cutting wages and cutting benefits.
• President Hindenburg took control of the Reichstag.
• The public saw the government as weak and started to look towards stronger leadership.

Quick Test

1. Why did the German public hate the War Guilt Clause so much?
2. Who were the 'November criminals'?
3. What did the government do in response to the economic issues of the early 1920s?
4. Give two reasons why the Great Depression was bad for the Weimar Republic.

Nazi rise to power, 1929–1933

Rise to power, to 1933

For much of the 1920s, the Nazis were a tiny minority party in the Reichstag. In 1928 they polled 2% of the overall vote. This all changed with the 1929 Wall Street Crash and ensuing Depression.

1930	• President Hindenburg ruled using Article 48. • The public lost faith in the government and turned to more extreme parties. • Communist support rose. Rich businessmen feared for their futures, so offered financial support to the Nazis. • 14 September – the Nazis polled over 18% of the vote.
1931	• Nazis increasingly popular, demonstrating organisation at a time of chaos, offering solutions to all Germany's problems. They deliberately disrupted Reichstag proceedings to make the government look weaker.
1932	• Hitler received 13 million votes in the Presidential election to Hindenburg's 19 million. • A series of weak Chancellors made Hitler look an increasingly viable candidate.

Date of Election	May 1928	Sep 1930	Jul 1932	Nov 1932	Mar 1933
Communists (KPD/USPD)	54	77	89	101	81
SPD (Social Democrats)	153	143	133	121	120
Centre Party (Catholics)	62	68	75	70	74
DDP (Democrats)	25	20	4	2	5
Right-wing parties (BVP/DVP/DNVP)	134	90	66	83	72
NSDAP (Nazis)	12	107	230	196	288
Others	51	72	11	12	7
Total Deputies	491	577	608	584	647

Election results 1928–1933

By 1933 Hindenburg was aged 85 and desperate. The Depression was deepening, the country was in chaos and there were few options left. As a result, Hitler was appointed Chancellor on 30 January 1933.

Consolidation of power, 1933–1934

In February 1933, the Reichstag building was set on fire. A Dutch Communist, van der Lubbe, was arrested and charged with starting the fire. That night, 4000 Communist leaders were arrested and imprisoned. Hitler persuaded Hindenburg to pass an emergency law suspending all the articles in the Constitution, including freedoms of speech, the press and assembly. The emergency law also:

- Gave police powers to search houses, confiscate property and detain people without trial.
- Decreed the death penalty for a wide range of crimes.
- Gave the police power to ban meetings, close newspapers, round up political opponents and send them to concentration camps

The public turned against the Communists and, in the March election, the Nazis achieved their best ever election results. However, they did not have an overall majority. Hitler realised that he would need even more drastic action.

The Nazis launched a campaign of propaganda showing how all other parties (especially the Communists) were a threat to Germany. Hitler filled the cabinet with Nazis and other supporters. The SA and SS bullied non-Nazis into supporting them. This gave Hitler the chance to pass more laws.

THINK POINT

There were short-term and long-term factors that led to Hitler becoming Führer. Which factor do you think was the most important? Can you support your answer?

Enabling Act, March 1933	Gave Hitler freedom to pass laws without consulting parliament. Made him legal dictator.
Power of local government destroyed	Meant that everything was controlled by the Nazis. Trade unions were banned.
Law against the Formation of New Parties – July 1933	SA attacked opposition parties' headquarters and arrested party members. Germany became a one party state.
Destroyed the legal system	Hitler set up the 'People's Court' which tried 'enemies of the state' for treason.

Three more steps ensured that Hitler had total control.

- The 'Night of the Long Knives' (29–30 June 1934). The SS arrested and executed Ernst Röhm and 400 SA members. This removed any opposition from within the Nazi party and guaranteed loyalty to Hitler.
- President Hindenburg died aged 86 (2 August 1934). Hitler merged the position of President and Chancellor.
- All members of the army swore an oath of loyalty to Hitler as Führer.

Quick Test

1. Give two reasons why the Nazis had grown in popularity by 1931.
2. How old was President Hindenburg when he appointed Hitler Chancellor?
3. Why was the Reichstag Fire important for the Nazis?
4. Why was the Enabling Act important for Hitler?

Nazi control

The structure of Nazi Germany was military and military-style obedience was required. Germany was no longer a democracy and there was no freedom of speech or association.

Who helped Hitler control Germany?

SA (or Brown Shirts)	• Paramilitary wing of the Nazi party, led by Ernst Röhm. • Helped introduce organisation in time of chaos and bullied opponents. • Purged in the Night of the Long Knives.
SS (or Black Shirts)	• Totally loyal bodyguards of Hitler. • Controlled intelligence, security and police forces. • Carried out the extermination of 'undesirables'. • Executed SA in the Night of the Long Knives.
Gestapo (Secret State Police)	• Aimed to eliminate political opponents. • Responsible for the rounding up of Jews during the Nazi regime.
'People's Courts'	• Set up to try opponents to the Nazi regime. • Resulted in thousands being sent to concentration camps.
Propaganda	• Nazis controlled newspapers, films and radio in order to spread their message. Josef Goebbels was in charge of Nazi propaganda. • Culminated in the annual Nuremberg Rallies.
Concentration camps	• Used in order to hold political prisoners and as a method of control. • Inmates were used as forced labour. Jews, criminals, homosexuals, gypsies, the mentally ill and others were sent there by 1939.

Treatment of Jews and other groups

1933	• Jewish shops attacked by SA troops. • April – one-day boycott of Jewish businesses. • Jewish doctors and dentists forbidden from working in state hospitals; Jewish lawyers and teachers sacked. • Non-Aryan editors removed from German newspapers. • Law passed to sterilise up to 350 000 men and women including Jews, gypsies, Jehovah's Witnesses and disabled people.
1934	• Special edition of *Der Stürmer* published reviving the accusation that Jews kill Christian children. • All homosexuals banned from military service.

TOP TIP

Look at some of the many Holocaust education websites to find out more about how the Nazis persecuted Jews and other opponents.

1935	• Jews and all non-Aryans excluded from military service. Jews prevented from becoming officers in the army.
	• The Nuremberg Laws passed
	– Jews and gypsies no longer citizens of Germany
	– Marriage and relationships between Aryans and non-Aryans forbidden.
1936	• Jewish families not entitled to state benefits (e.g. child allowance).
	• 400 gypsies taken to Dachau concentration camp.
1937	• Jews banned from working in any government or political role.
1938	• Red 'J' stamped on all Jewish passports.
	• Kristallnacht
	– 1000 synagogues set alight; 7000 Jewish businesses destroyed
	– 20 000 Jews sent to concentration camps
	– Nearly 100 Jewish men murdered.
1939	• Law passed to allow Jews to be taken to camps for forced labour.
	• October – first Jewish ghetto established.
	• 3000 gypsies sent to concentration camps.

Opposition in Nazi Germany

Socialists were one of the largest groups to speak out. Many socialists were employed by the state, so were dealt with through the Enabling Act. They struggled in the face of SA/SS force and refused to collaborate with the Communists, so any real threat was reduced.

Communists also opposed the Nazis, but with little success. Many were arrested and executed after the Reichstag Fire and the party was banned by the end of 1933.

The Church influenced the German public and was therefore seen as a more serious threat to Nazi control. Hitler knew that crushing the Church would be unpopular, so tried to work with them:

- *Concordat* with Catholic Church signed in 1933, guaranteeing each side would stay out of the other's business.
- Protestant churches joined together in one official *Reich Church* in September 1933.
- *National Reich Church* set up in November 1933. *Mein Kampf* replaced the Bible and the Swastika replaced the cross.

Bishop Galen and Pastor Martin Niemöller were two church leaders who spoke out. Niemöller was arrested and put in solitary confinement for seven years.

Quick Test

1. What were the methods of control in Nazi Germany?
2. What were the Nuremberg Laws?
3. Who was in charge of propaganda?
4. What happened to Pastor Niemöller?

Nazi social and economic policies

Methods to ensure support from ordinary people

Throughout the Nazi regime, it was clear that winning the public over was the main way to maintain control. Thus, Hitler aimed to keep the people on his side through delivering on his promise to make Germany a great nation again.

- The Nazis aimed for full employment through suspending reparation repayments, reinvesting the money in German companies and making Germany self-sustaining. Thousands were employed by the government building hospitals, schools and motorways. National Service employed all able young men for a time. Women and Jews were sacked, so there were more jobs for 'real' German men. Hitler ignored the Treaty of Versailles and rearmament created jobs in industry.

- There was financial help for families. For example, money was given for couples to marry (a loan of 1000 marks) and each child born was given 250 marks.

- Hitler believed that militarism was the key to success. It was essential that Germany should have a strong leader. This was the 'Führer Prinzip' – one person should have all the power to make all the decisions. All Germans had to learn to trust and obey the Führer without thinking. People had to ignore their own self-interests and put Germany before themselves. They had to be willing to suffer or sacrifice themselves if it benefited Germany. The importance of war was highlighted, as Hitler wanted people to believe that only through war could the Master Race expand and get *Lebensraum* (living space).

A poster for the League of German Girls

- The Nuremberg Rallies were held every summer and were a chance for Hitler to show his military power to Germans and to the rest of the world. The rallies took place in the Nuremberg Arena and included fireworks displays, torch lit processions and military marches. The highlight of the week of rallies was Hitler's speech, in which Hitler appeared like a military god. The rallies displayed the Nazis' military values and might.

DID YOU KNOW?

Schemes were launched in order to help German citizens and increase Nazi popularity. For example, Volkswagen cars, camps and cruises were offered at a reduced rate. Rewards such as these are often called the 'carrot' when punishments are the 'stick'. Draw a diagram showing how the Nazis controlled the German people by using rewards and punishments.

How did the Nazis control the young?

Hitler believed that the Nazi regime could only be sustained by bringing up young Germans to be 'good' Nazis. Youth organisations and education were a key part of controlling the Nazi future.

The Hitler Youth movements were set up in 1925 and by 1936 there were over four million members. All other youth organisations were banned. The youth organisations were key in controlling the rest of the population. Members were encouraged to inform their leaders about other children and adults who were not living in the 'Nazi way'.

Boys	Girls
The army of the future in order to secure a 'Thousand Year Reich'.	Expected to provide future generations of soldiers and to ensure that children were brought up in the 'Nazi way'.
Expected to join the Hitler Youth from the ages of 14 to 18. Prior to that were the 'Little Fellows' from 6–10 and the 'Youth Folk' from 14–18.	Expected to join the League of German Maidens.
Encouraged to learn military techniques and take part in military training.	Encouraged to take part in physical activity in order to make them fit for motherhood.

How did the Nazis control education?

Schools were to follow Nazi ideology, with any opposition teachers removed very quickly. Pupils were brainwashed at any opportunity. Maths textbooks referred to bombing of Jewish ghettos and asked pupils to calculate the cost of keeping mentally ill Germans alive.

Schools had the military discipline of the youth movements. Head teachers were given more power to punish pupils and complete obedience was expected from all. Physical Education and History were key subjects for boys, while girls studied Eugenics (racial science) and Home Economics, which included motherhood and bringing up children.

Teacher points to Danzig explaining its strategic importance to the Nazis

Quick Test

1. Give three examples of ways in which Hitler increased male employment.
2. What was the purpose of the Hitler Youth movements?
3. What subjects did girls focus on at school?
4. How was education altered to deliver the Nazi message?

Timeline

1918 – Kaiser abdicates and First World War is over.

1919 – Spartacist Revolt.

1923 – Munich Beerhall Putsch.

1929 – Wall Street Crash and the beginning of the Great Depression.

January 1933 – Hitler appointed Chancellor of Germany.

February 1933 – Reichstag Fire.

June 1934 – Night of the Long Knives.

August 1934 – Death of President Hindenburg.

1935 – Nuremberg Laws introduced.

1938 – Kristallnacht.

1939 – First Jewish ghetto established.

Biographies

Adolf Hitler (1889–1945)

Born in Austria, Hitler became leader of Germany in 1933 and ruled until he committed suicide in 1945. He was a failed artist, a soldier in the First World War and leader of the Nazi party from 1921. Hitler was a skilled public speaker and strong leader. He held very strong anti-Semitic beliefs and saw it as his mission to rid Europe of Jews and make Germany great again. He sought revenge for the loss of the First World War and believed that the German people were destined to dominate Europe.

Josef Goebbels (1897–1945)

Goebbels was in charge of propaganda in Nazi Germany from 1933–1945. Through his aggressive use of propaganda, he made Hitler and the Nazis appear to be the only solution to Germany's problems. He campaigned against the Socialists and Communists as well as Jews. From 1933 he had total control over all areas of the media. He produced several anti-Semitic films and was responsible for the events of Kristallnacht. Goebbels committed suicide at the end of the Second World War.

Heinrich Himmler (1900–1945)

Himmler was a member of the Nazi party from the early 1920s, having served as a soldier in the First World War. He became head of the SS in 1929 and was elected to the Reichstag in 1930. He became head of the police state in Nazi Germany and set up the first concentration camp in Dachau in 1933. He was in charge of making Germany 'racially pure' and he oversaw the attempt to exterminate all Jews in Europe. Himmler was captured by the Allies at the end of the Second World War, but committed suicide while in custody.

Paul von Hindenburg (1847–1934)

Hindenburg served as Germany's President from 1925 to his death in 1934. He was a First World War hero and remained President throughout some of Germany's most difficult times. He appointed Hitler in 1933 through desperation. A series of failed governments had left him with little choice. When Hindenburg died, Hitler merged the posts of Chancellor and President.

Friedrich (Martin) Niemöller (1892–1984)

Pastor Niemöller was a sailor in the German Navy during the First World War. When the war ended, Niemöller became a preacher. He rejected the new Weimar government and supported some of the right-wing parties in Germany. Initially, he spoke favourably about Hitler and the Nazi Party, but later was very outspoken in his criticism of their anti-Jewish policies and founded the Confessional Church. He was imprisoned in Dachau and Sachsenhausen concentration camps from 1937–1945.

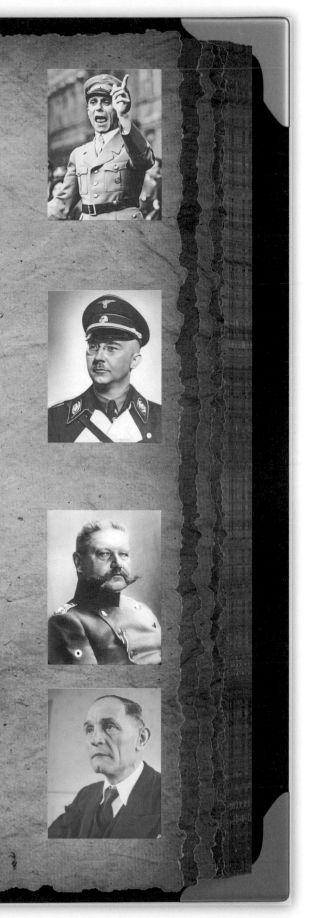

Immigration to 1928

Throughout the nineteenth century, the USA had an 'open door' policy towards immigration. Immigrants were welcome to make their fortune in the 'New World'.

The USA at the end of the First World War

By 1920 the population of the USA had grown to over 100 million people, with thousands flooding in through this 'open door'.

At first, the majority were from north-west Europe (Britain, France, Germany and Scandinavia). These 'old immigrants' were White Anglo-Saxon Protestants (WASPs). 'New immigrants' from Poland, Italy and Russia started arriving by 1900. By the end of the First World War there were more 'new immigrants' from India, China, Japan, Africa and the Middle East.

With the First World War far away in Europe (America joined the war late in 1917), the USA had escaped the worst of the horrors of war. Industry

Immigrants at Ellis Island

and agriculture grew and America replaced Britain as the 'workshop of the world'. It was an attractive country with a good climate, plenty of jobs and a welcome for all immigrants. It was a place where hard work would be rewarded with riches – a place where you could live the 'American Dream'.

What was the status of the ethnic groups in the USA?

New immigrants – the first wave

The first wave of new immigrants faced fewer issues than other ethnic minorities. Initially they were welcomed into American society, but hostility grew as their numbers increased and they were accused of stealing jobs. The Second World War raised awareness of them being outsiders and there was significant hostility, especially towards Italians (and Germans).

These new immigrants tended to settle in cheaper areas of housing in the cities. The Jewish and Roman Catholic immigrants were targeted by the KKK from 1915 and were accused of being Communists.

They were never denied political rights and so were able to make more progress than other minorities. They were able to integrate more fully into American society due to their physical appearance and the colour of their skin.

Hispanics

They lived in *barrios* – slum areas with poor living conditions. They were separated by language and religion. They often worked in very poorly paid agricultural jobs and were seen by white Americans to be stealing jobs and lowering wages.

Asians

Asians arrived in huge numbers from the mid-nineteenth century due to the discovery of gold in California and faced significant discrimination. There were anti-Chinese riots in San Francisco as early as 1877.

They faced significant hostility during the Second World War when Japan and the USA fought over the Pacific. Much of the Japanese population in America was put in concentration camps.

Native Americans

The tribes of Native Americans historically conflicted with white Americans. They lost large areas of land and were forcibly removed from prosperous areas and moved to reservations. They were denied the right to vote and were not granted citizenship of the USA until 1924.

Black Americans

At the bottom of the racial hierarchy due to the history of slavery in the USA, black Americans faced 'de jure' (legal) segregation in the south. Separate facilities and schools existed and overt racial abuse was common.

They faced 'de facto' (not legal, but happened all the same) segregation in the North. Living in the poorest ghettos of the northern cities, black Americans had very few educational opportunities and they often worked in the poorest paid jobs.

THINK POINT

If you have ever moved home, what has been the reason? Do you know if your ancestors moved? The Ellis Island website is excellent and you can find out whether any of your ancestors emigrated to America.

Quick Test

1. What does 'WASP' stand for?
2. Where did most new immigrants come from?
3. Why was the Second World War important for new immigrants?
4. What is the difference between 'de jure' and 'de facto'?

'Separate but equal', to 1939

'Jim Crow Laws'

'Jim Crow Laws' were introduced between 1870 and 1900; one of the best known is the 'Separate but Equal' Act of 1876.

- Black children were forbidden to attend schools with white children.
- Black Americans had restricted access to parks and restaurants.
- Black Americans were not allowed to marry white Americans.
- There were even separate graveyards and bathrooms.

These laws basically made racism in the south legal and made it very difficult for black Americans to improve their situation.

Segregated drinking fountain

How did attitudes towards immigration change in the 1920s?

In the early 1920s two key laws were passed that illustrate the changing attitude of Americans towards immigration.

1921 Emergency Immigration Act

- Introduced a quota that severely restricted immigration from non-WASP countries. Under the quota system 80% of those entering came from Britain, Ireland, Germany, Holland, Switzerland and Scandinavia.

1924 National Origins Act

- Set an absolute limit of 150 000 immigrants per annum and sharply restricted immigration from the south and east of Europe and Asia.

Why did attitudes towards immigration change in the 1920s?

The nature of immigration changed

By the end of the nineteenth century, the number of new immigrants arriving was greater than the number of old immigrants. This threatened the WASP way of life. Also, many of the new immigrants were Roman Catholic or Jewish, which threatened the Protestant establishment. Many came from non-democratic countries. This was seen as a threat to the US Constitution. Most did not speak English and so were seen to be less intelligent.

First World War

The First World War had led to hostility towards anything foreign and in 1917 the US closed its borders to immigrants. War created tension with the large German-American population. Italians were also targeted and anti-Japanese racism peaked at this time.

Internal conditions

WASPs feared that the number of immigrants would threaten employment, education and housing. The new immigrants' willingness to work for very low wages led to tension, as they were often used as strike - breakers.

Attitudes towards immigration changed as a result of a combination of factors. However, it is clear that the threat felt by the WASP establishment is the key to explaining the restriction on immigration. As a result of this threat, some started to look for extreme solutions to problems of immigration and extreme violent organisations like the KKK re-emerged.

What was the Ku Klux Klan?

- Based mainly in the southern states.
- Often members were policemen, lawyers, judges and politicians, which made them difficult to oppose. Influential votes would be lost if the government acted against them.
- Dressed in white robes and hooded masks; used the burning cross as a symbol.
- Lynched black Americans they thought were trying to challenge the status quo; prevented black Americans from voting in elections.

KKK march in New Jersey

Many black Americans moved to the northern cities to escape persecution. KKK activity moved north as a result of this 'Great Migration'.

What was the impact of KKK activity?

- Ensured black Americans were unable to change the situation in the southern states.
- Ensured that segregation and racial abuse carried on.
- Kept up pressure on the government not to introduce change.

> ### TOP TIP
> The activities of the KKK are often seen as a cause of discrimination. Actually, the KKK is a symptom of discrimination already in place. Some historians argue that WASPs feared for their status in America, so the violence, including murder, beatings and arson, was a reaction to that fear.

Quick Test

1. Which groups of immigrants were restricted in the 1920s?
2. In what ways did the First World War have an impact on immigration?
3. What steps did the KKK take in order to maintain WASP superiority?
4. Why would the government not want to stop the KKK?

Civil rights movement, 1945–1964

Why did the civil rights movement grow at this time?

Impact of the Second World War

Black American soldiers talked about the 'Double-V-Campaign': victory in the war and victory for civil rights at home. Philip Randolf (an early leader in the movement) demanded an end to segregation in the armed forces. Executive order 8802 achieved this.

Organised resistance

Despite some improvement in black Americans' civil rights, the Jim Crow Laws continued across the south. Discrimination after the Second World War meant that an organised movement was needed in order to improve the situation.

Two key areas demonstrate the link between the discrimination and an organised movement:

Education:

- 1954 – Brown v Board of Education of Topeka. The NAACP supported the case that tried to allow a black child to go to a 'white' school.

- 1957 – Little Rock Central High School. The NAACP supported nine black students in their attempt to go to Little Rock Central High School.

Protest against the integration of Little Rock High School, 1959

Transport:

- 1955 – Rosa Parks and the Montgomery Bus Boycott. This started with Rosa Parks refusing to give up her seat on a bus for a white person. Supported by the NAACP, there was an organised bus boycott in Montgomery. This resulted in buses being desegregated.

Public awareness

Two key events attracted much publicity:

Emmett Till murder (1955)

- 14 year old Emmett Till was brutally murdered for speaking to a white woman in Mississippi. Pictures of his beaten body sparked outrage.

- The case attracted widespread publicity and proved just how much an organised civil rights movement was needed.

Birmingham Sunday School bombing (1963)

- Four children were killed by a large explosion in a Baptist Church.

- Following the bombing there were violent clashes between protestors and the police.

- Again this violence against black Americans made the call for civil rights louder.

Emergence of effective black leaders

The best known of these leaders was Martin Luther King. King believed that non-violence was the key to achieving civil rights. He was an inspirational leader, great organiser and powerful speaker. He led boycotts, sit-ins, freedom rides and marches, such as the 300 000 strong march on Washington.

Effective black organisations formed

- NAACP – key in many of the early protests.
- SCLC – organised march on Washington and protests in Birmingham.
- The Student Nonviolent Coordinating Committee (SNCC) – played a major role in organising sit-ins and freedom rides.
- CORE – also helped organise the march on Washington and the freedom rides.

What was the Federal and state response?

- Peaceful actions were met with violent retaliation.
- Leaders such as Bull Connor and Governor Wallace used clubs, fire hoses and police dogs to control the protestors.
- President Kennedy reacted by introducing the 1964 Civil Rights Act.

What was the impact on US society?

The combined efforts of civil rights groups ultimately resulted in the 1964 Civil Rights Act which granted:

- Equal voting rights for black Americans.
- An end to discrimination on the basis of colour of skin in public buildings and the workplace.
- An end to segregated public schools.

However:

- Racism was still widespread across the southern states.
- King wanted further change.
- Very few black Americans had succeeded in registering to vote (especially in Alabama).

> **DID YOU KNOW?**
>
> Some of the first civil rights leaders like Marcus Garvey suggested that the best way to improve the position of black Americans was to leave America and return to Africa.

Quick Test

1. What was the 'Double-V-Campaign'?
2. Why were cases like the murder of Emmett Till important?
3. What did Martin Luther King believe would bring about change?
4. Why was the 1964 Civil Rights Act important for black Americans?

Ghettos and black American radicalism

What were ghettos?

Most black Americans lived in run-down, slum areas of the cities, known as ghettos.

The ghettos grew as a result of the Great Migration in the 1950s and 1960s. Thousands of black Americans moved north to escape the problems in the southern states and to find homes and jobs in the northern cities.

Race riots

Watts, Los Angeles (1965)

- The population was 98% black, but the police force was almost entirely white.
- The black population was growing impatient with the lack of progress of the civil rights movement, unemployment was high and poverty was reaching an unbearable state.
- A fight broke out which grew into a confrontation between police and black residents of Watts. The riots lasted for six days and left 34 dead, 900 wounded and 4000 arrested.

Watts riots, 1965

Chicago (1966)

- On 12 July police shut down a fire hydrant that had been opened by black teenagers wanting to cool down.
- A fight broke out in which ten people were injured, windows were smashed and some shops were looted.
- The next night saw sniper fire, petrol bombs and the stoning of city firemen.

Long hot summers (1966–1967)

- There were 43 race riots in 1966 and 159 in 1967.
- Black Americans in the northern cities were beginning to lose faith in non-violent protest and started to look to new leaders.

The Northern civil rights movement

By the middle of the 1960s the civil rights movement was changing. Non-violence was becoming less popular and the northern cities wanted change. They looked towards more extreme leaders like Malcolm X and Stokely Carmichael.

Malcolm X's beliefs

- White and black societies should be totally separate.
- He was prepared to use violence.
- He showed hatred towards the white 'devils' in his speeches.

Stokely Carmichael

- Elected national chairman of SNCC in June 1966.
- He was an advocate of black supremacy and 'black power'.
- He left the SNCC in 1968 to join an even more extreme group called the *Black Panthers*.

> **TOP TIP**
>
> It is important to look at the differences between the movement in the north and in the south. Draw a table showing the differing views of Martin Luther King and Malcolm X.

How did the government respond to radical protest?

The government launched an investigation into the violence and rioting. It was led by Otto Kerner, who discovered several things that shocked the nation.

- USA was divided into two societies – one black and poor, the other white and richer.
- 40% of all black Americans lived in poverty and this was the reason for the riots.
- Black men were twice as likely to be unemployed as white men.
- Black men were three times as likely to be in low skilled jobs as white men.

What was the reaction to Kerner's findings?

Little was done in response to most of the findings of the Commission, but there was a significant step forward in regard to one of the major conclusions.

The new Civil Rights Act of 1968 was passed in direct response to the problem of poverty and acknowledged that there was a definite link between poverty and housing.

Quick Test

1. Why did black Americans move north in the Great Migration?
2. In which cities were there race riots in the 1960s?
3. What did Malcolm X believe would bring about change?
4. Why did the Kerner report shock people?

Timeline

1921 – Emergency Immigration Act passed.

1924 – Native Americans granted American citizenship.

1954 – Brown *v* Board of Education of Topeka.

1955 – Rosa Parks and the beginning of the bus boycotts in Alabama.

1957 – Little Rock High School.

1963 – March on Washington and the 'I have a dream' speech.

1964 – Civil Rights Act passed.

1965 – Malcolm X assassinated.

1968 – Martin Luther King Jr. assassinated.

1968 – Civil Rights Act passed.

Biographies

Martin Luther King Jr. (1929–1968)

Martin Luther King Jr. was probably the most famous civil rights leader anywhere in the world. He was a Baptist minister and winner of the Nobel Peace Prize in 1964. He was a key organiser of many of the civil rights movement's most important protests, such as the march on Washington in 1963. He also protested against the war in Vietnam, as it was against his belief in non-violence. King was assassinated in 1968.

Malcolm X (1925–1965)

Born Malcolm Little, he changed his surname to 'X' as a symbol of his slave ancestry. He converted to Islam after a spell in prison in the early 1950s. He later spoke of his regret about some of his actions as part of the 'Nation of Islam'. His speeches were full of suggestions that white people were the devil who should be kept separate from black society. Malcolm X was assassinated in 1965.

Stokely Carmichael (1941–1998)

Born in Trinidad in the Caribbean, Carmichael became an important civil rights leader working with Martin Luther King in the southern states. He later lost faith in non-violent tactics and moved towards the 'black power' movement, becoming associated with the violent Black Panthers. Carmichael left America in 1969 and lived the rest of his life in north-west Africa.

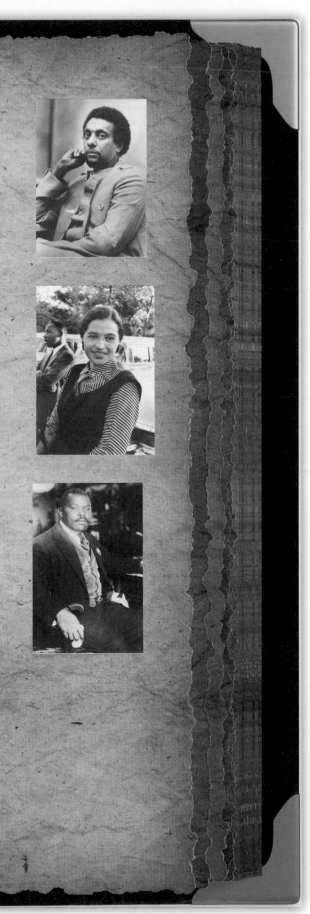

Rosa Parks (1913–2005)

Rosa Parks was a civil rights leader most famous for being arrested for refusing to give up her seat on a public bus in Montgomery, Alabama. She was supported by the NAACP and there followed a series of bus boycotts across the city. This was a key moment in the civil rights movement and involved Martin Luther King. Parks lived most of her life in Detroit working as a secretary to an African-American politician.

Marcus Garvey (1887–1940)

Garvey was a Jamaican born activist most famous for his 'Back to Africa' campaign. Garvey was highly intelligent and a talented public speaker. He formed the Universal Negro Improvement Association (UNIA) in 1914 and soon developed a reputation as a strong and inspirational leader. He founded the Black Star Line as a transport company to help black Americans return to Africa.

Reasons for the emergence of the Cold War

The Cold War is the name given to the period from 1945 to 1989 when suspicion and rivalry between the USA and her allies and the Soviet Union and her allies threatened armed conflict.

The Iron Curtain

In a speech in 1946, the former British Prime Minister, Winston Churchill, talked about an 'Iron Curtain', an imaginary barrier between the democratic countries in the West and the Soviet dominated communist countries in the East. The phrase meant that the East and West were deeply divided by different beliefs.

Capitalism: USA	Communism: Soviet Union
Industries/businesses privately owned	Industries/businesses owned by the state
Individual ambition and the creation of wealth encouraged	Wealth shared equally
Choice of several political parties	One party state – only the Communist Party allowed
Free speech and debate	Only communist ideas promoted. Government cannot be challenged.

TOP TIP

Become familiar with the terms that relate to the Cold War. An understanding and the correct use of terms such as communism and capitalism will impress an examiner.

Reasons for breakdown of relations

TOP TIP

Political terms relating to the Soviet Union can be tricky. Background reading on twentieth century Russian history will help you understand your study of the Cold War, e.g. the Red Flag chapter.

- Stalin created a buffer zone of communist countries to prevent the USSR from being attacked. By 1948 the USSR controlled almost all of Eastern Europe.
- **Truman Doctrine:** proposed that the USA would lend money to any country to fight communism.
- **Marshall Plan:** offered aid to European countries to rebuild after the war.
- **Berlin airlift:** In 1945 the British, Americans, French and the Russians each controlled one area or zone of Germany. The capital, Berlin, which was inside the Russian zone, was also divided into four zones. In 1948 Stalin ordered the blockade of all roads, railways and canals leading into West Berlin. American and British planes flew in supplies to keep the people in West Berlin alive. The Berlin airlift was a turning point in the relationship between East and West. The Western powers joined their zones to form the Federal Republic of Germany or West Germany while the Russian zone became the German Democratic Republic or East Germany.

- Two alliance systems developed. In 1949 a number of Western nations set up the **North Atlantic Treaty Organisation** (NATO) to protect them from the USSR. If one member was attacked the other members would help them. The Soviet Union and its Eastern European allies responded with a similar alliance in 1955 called the **Warsaw Pact**.

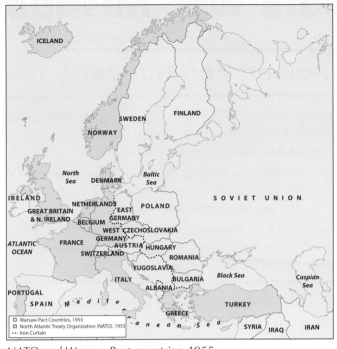

NATO and Warsaw Pact countries, 1955

Military rivalry

Due to mutual suspicion each side built more weapons. Both the United States and the Soviet Union increased the size of their armies and air forces. The arms race became more dangerous when each side began to develop bigger and more destructive nuclear weapons. The build-up of nuclear arms increased tensions even more.

The Arms Race	
1945	USA drops two atomic bombs (A-bombs) on Hiroshima and Nagasaki in Japan.
1949	Soviet Union explodes its first A-bomb.
1952	USA explodes a hydrogen bomb (H-bomb).
1955	Soviet Union tests its first hydrogen bomb.
1957	Soviet Union tests its first intercontinental ballistic missile (ICBM) capable of carrying a nuclear missile.

The Cold War now had the potential to turn into a devastating world war. A state of mutually assured destruction (MAD) had been reached.

Quick Test

1. What was the 'Cold War'?
2. What action was taken by Stalin to prevent the Soviet Union from being attacked?
3. What event marked a turning point in the relationship between the East and the West?
4. What was the aim of the North Atlantic Treaty Organisation?

Cold War flashpoints

Poland and Hungary, 1956

Stalin died in 1953 and Nikita Khrushchev became the new leader of the Soviet Union. In 1956 Khrushchev criticised Stalin's rule. Some Warsaw Pact countries hoped there might be a relaxation of Soviet control.

- Workers in Poland protested against Soviet domination and demanded political reform. The demonstrations were suppressed but Poland gained some reforms as long as they remained loyal to the USSR.

- There were also demands for reform in Hungary culminating in Imre Nagy's threat to leave the Warsaw Pact. Soviet tanks entered Budapest to put down the uprising. Around 20 000 Hungarian people were killed and thousands fled abroad.

Berlin

A divided Berlin presented problems for the USSR:

- It was the only place in Eastern Europe where people in communist countries had contact with the West. East Berliners saw that West Berliners had a higher standard of living and more freedoms.

- Many East Germans moved to the West through Berlin. Many were skilled workers, which created a labour shortage in East Germany.

In 1961, Khrushchev ordered the building of a wall to cut Berlin in two with barbed wire and guard towers to prevent anyone escaping to the West. The 'Iron Curtain' was now a physical reality.

The West protested and sent extra troops to West Berlin. However, the possibility of war had been reduced between the two superpowers.

- The flood of refugees from the East came to a halt although people still tried to escape and were killed in the attempt.

- The Soviet Union abandoned its attempts to force Western troops out of Berlin.

Construction of the Berlin Wall

Cuba, 1962

- In 1959 Batista was overthrown by revolutionaries led by Fidel Castro. The USA imposed sanctions after Castro took control of American businesses in Cuba.
- US President Kennedy approved a CIA plan for an invasion at the Bay of Pigs. The invasion was a failure and humiliated Kennedy.
- Castro formed an alliance with the Soviet Union.
- On 16 October 1962 a US spy plane revealed evidence of Soviet missile launch sites being built on Cuba.
- On 22 October the USA imposed a naval blockade of Cuba to prevent Soviet ships landing missiles.
- Kennedy stated that a missile attack from Cuba would result in a full scale attack by the USA on the USSR.
- Kennedy began to mobilise troops for a possible invasion of Cuba. The world feared a nuclear war between the two superpowers.

The crisis came to an end on 28 October.

- Secret negotiations were held between Kennedy and Khrushchev.
- Despite a US spy plane being shot down over Cuba and the US navy searching a Soviet merchant ship for missiles, neither side took action.
- Kennedy ended the blockade and promised not to invade Cuba.
- In a secret deal between the two leaders, the Soviet Union agreed to remove their missiles from Cuba in exchange for the removal of US missiles from Britain, Italy and Turkey.

The Cuban Missile Crisis had an important impact on international relations and led to a thaw in the Cold War.

- Telephone 'hot line' between Washington and Moscow set up in 1963.
- Test Ban Treaty signed, agreeing to stop all nuclear tests in the air, under water or in space.

Quick Test

1. Who replaced Stalin as the new leader of the Soviet Union?
2. Why did Soviet troops move into Budapest?
3. Why did the Soviet Union order a wall to be built separating East and West Berlin?
4. What actions were taken by the USA after evidence was discovered of the presence of Soviet missiles on Cuba?

The Vietnam War

Reasons for United States' involvement

In 1954, the people of Vietnam won their freedom from French rule. The north became a communist republic under the control of the Viet Minh, led by Ho Chi Minh. The south became an anti-communist republic under Ngo Dinh Diem. In the late 1950s communist *guerrillas* (the Vietcong) in South Vietnam began fighting Diem's government which was unpopular and corrupt. North Vietnam sent weapons and soldiers to help the Vietcong while the United States sent weapons and advisers to the South Vietnamese. By 1964 the USA had become involved in a full scale war. The main reasons were:

The domino theory

- The situation in Vietnam provided an opportunity to make a stand against communism.
- The USA believed in the 'domino theory'. This was the belief that if South Vietnam fell to the communists, other countries would follow suit.
- North Vietnam received help from China and the USSR. The USA feared the possibility of a new communist superpower bloc.

Reasons for the failure to defeat the Vietcong

By 1973 US troops had withdrawn from Vietnam, ultimately unable to defeat the Vietcong. The reasons for this were:

- The Vietcong were experienced in guerrilla tactics. They were also hard to spot as they did not wear uniforms and lived among the peasants.
- The North Vietnamese built the Ho Chi Minh Trail to supply South Vietnam with troops and equipment.
- In contrast, American tactics proved ineffective.
- American soldiers were not trained or equipped for jungle warfare. Low morale sometimes resulted in excessive drinking and drug use. Due to the draft system the American army mainly consisted of inexperienced young conscripts.

The Ho Chi Minh Trail

Tactic	Reasons for failure
Bombing of strategic targets such as army bases and railways.	Bombs often missed their targets. Children and hospital patients were among those killed.
Peasants were moved from their villages and placed in **strategic hamlets** to prevent contact with the Vietcong.	Resulted in the Vietnamese peasants hating the Americans.
Chemical bombs including **napalm** were used to destroy trees in the jungle.	Innocent civilians, men, women and children, were burned by napalm.

Changing views on the war in the USA

Why did the Vietnam War become increasingly unpopular in the United States?

- It was costing billions of dollars. Hundreds of thousands of American soldiers lost their lives. Television coverage showed the full horrors of the war. The American people became demoralised by atrocities such as the My Lai massacre.
- Tactics such as the use of napalm and Agent Orange turned people against the war.

How did the American people show their opposition to the Vietnam War?

- Large demonstrations and student protests
- Draft dodging
- Vietnam veterans and famous figures such as Mohammed Ali and Martin Luther King spoke out against the war
- Anti-Vietnam songs were popular.

Impact of the Vietnam War on international relations

In 1975 South Vietnam was invaded and defeated by North Vietnam. Vietnam was unified as a single communist country. American involvement in Vietnam was largely seen as a failure, not only by the American public but internationally.

TOP TIP

Although Laos and Cambodia became communist, other countries in South East Asia, such as Thailand, did not. The domino theory had been proved wrong. Some people argue that the domino theory was just an excuse for the USA to increase its power.

Quick Test

1.	What was the 'domino theory'?
2.	What was the Ho Chi Minh Trail?
3.	Why was there low morale among American soldiers?
4.	Why did public opinion in America turn against involvement in Vietnam?

Changing relations between the superpowers, 1968–1989

Attempts at détente

Throughout the 1960s and 1970s the USA and the USSR tried to put aside their differences. They formed a détente, or understanding, with each other which reduced tension and the threat of war. The reasons for the changing attitudes between the USA and the USSR were:

- The Cuban Missile Crisis had shown how close they had come to nuclear war.
- Better relations meant fewer weapons needed to be built. This allowed Western and Eastern leaders to portray themselves as peacemakers and increase their popularity. There were anti-nuclear demonstrations in a number of countries.
- The USA had economic problems. Money spent on nuclear weapons meant there was less available to improve living conditions.
- The USSR also faced economic problems. It was spending 20% of its budget on defence. Its industry was also very inefficient compared with American industry. Soviet industry had to improve before people's standards of living could rise.
- The USSR had begun to quarrel with communist China.

Several agreements were made to improve relations between the USA and the Soviet Union.

- In 1972 the SALT I Treaty led to a reduction of nuclear weapons.
- In 1975, 33 European countries signed the Helsinki Agreement confirming the existing borders of Europe.

There were also trade links between the superpowers and co-operation over space missions.

Setbacks

However, a number of events led to the breakdown of détente by the late 1970s and early 1980s.

- In 1979 Soviet forces invaded Afghanistan
- In 1980 the new American President, Ronald Reagan, referred to the Soviet Union as 'the evil empire'.
- The USA boycotted the Olympic Games in Moscow in 1980 and the Soviet Union boycotted the 1984 Los Angeles Olympic Games
- The USA increased its defence budget and announced the Strategic Defence Initiative which proposed satellite systems which would be able to shoot down Soviet missiles before they hit their target.

End of the Cold War

In 1985 Mikhail Gorbachev took power in the Soviet Union. Gorbachev wanted to reform communism and address the social, economic and political problems within the Soviet Union. He proposed to do this through a combination of:

Germans on top of the Berlin Wall as it is torn down

- **Glasnost** meaning openness or a free exchange of ideas and information. The press had more freedom, criticism of the government was tolerated and previously banned books could be read.

- **Perestroika** meaning a reconstruction of the entire Soviet system. Gorbachev relaxed state control of industry in the hope that the Soviet economy would become more productive.

In 1987 a landmark agreement between the Soviet Union and the USA removed all nuclear missiles from Europe and reduced the number of ICBM missiles. This agreement effectively brought the arms race to an end.

Gorbachev also began to change the Soviet Union's role in Eastern Europe. Warsaw Pact countries were given more independence. By 1989 several European countries had rejected communism. In November 1989 the Berlin Wall was torn down. This was a key moment in the history of Europe and symbolised the end of the Cold War.

THINK POINT

Was the Cold War a struggle between different belief systems, Communism and Capitalism, or was it a struggle for power? Historians continue to debate explanations for the Cold War between the East and the West from 1945 to 1989.

Quick Test

1. What was meant by 'détente'?
2. What actions were taken by the superpowers to improve relations?
3. Who was the American president who referred to the Soviet Union as an 'evil empire'?
4. What were Gorbachev's two ideas for reforming communism?

Timeline

May 1945 – The Second World War in Europe comes to an end.

12 March 1947 – US President Truman promises to resist communism.

29 August 1949 – The Soviet Union carries out its first atom bomb test.

1 November 1952 – The USA explodes its first hydrogen bomb.

4 November 1956 – Soviet troops invade Hungary to suppress an anti-communist uprising.

12–13 August 1961 – Construction of the Berlin Wall begins, dividing the city in two.

October 1962 – The Cuban Missile Crisis brings the world to the brink of nuclear war.

8 March 1965 – The USA sends marines to fight communist-led guerrillas in Vietnam.

8 December 1987 – The signing of a nuclear arms treaty signals the end of hostile relations between the USA and the Soviet Union.

9 November 1989 – Gates in the Berlin Wall are opened as communism collapses in Eastern Europe.

Biographies

Mikhail Gorbachev (1931–)

Mikhail Gorbachev was leader of the Soviet Union from 1985 to 1991. He came to agreements with the USA to reduce the numbers of nuclear weapons and withdrew Soviet forces from Eastern European countries and Afghanistan. Two of his most important policies were *perestroika* (restructuring) and *glasnost* (openness).

Ronald Reagan (1911–2004)

US President from 1980 to 1988, Reagan was determined to stand up to the Soviet Union. Reagan increased American spending on nuclear missiles. His policy towards the Soviet Union changed in the late 1980s when he met with Mikhail Gorbachev to discuss limiting the number of nuclear weapons countries owned.

Nikita Khrushchev (1895–1971)

Khrushchev was the leader of the Soviet Union from 1953 to 1964. In 1956 he criticised Stalin at a Communist Party congress. In 1962 he placed Soviet nuclear missiles on the island of Cuba which brought the USA and the Soviet Union close to war.

John F. Kennedy (1917–1963)

Kennedy was US President from 1960 until his assassination in 1963. He took a tough line towards the Soviet Union over West Berlin. In 1962 he negotiated with Khrushchev to avoid a nuclear conflict during the Cuban Missile Crisis.

Joseph Stalin (1879–1953)

Stalin was Soviet leader from 1929 to 1953. Stalin's brutal dictatorship of the Soviet Union led to the deaths of millions of Soviet citizens. After 1945 Stalin extended Soviet influence to Eastern Europe. In 1948–49 Stalin tried to remove the Western allies from West Berlin through the Berlin blockade.

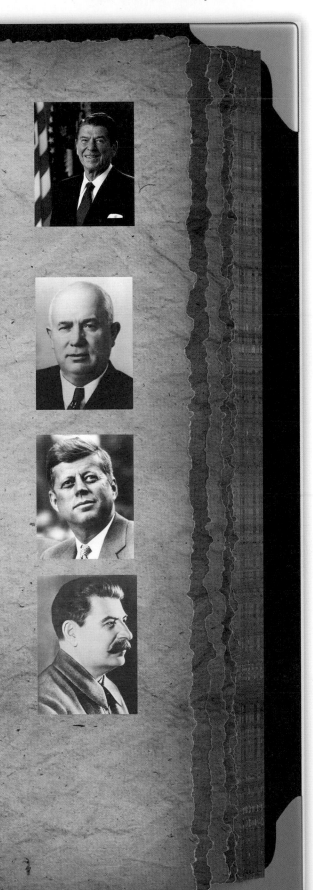

Exam skills

Describe question

Describe questions are designed to test your knowledge and understanding of an event or the results of an event. The questions should be relatively straightforward as long as you have done some revision before trying to answer the question. The question usually starts with the words 'Describe …' or 'What …?'. For example,

'Describe the sort of jobs done by Irish immigrants in Scotland.'

OR

'What were the results of the 1923 economic crisis for the German people?'

Key points

- These questions are worth 5 or 6 marks.
- One relevant point = one sentence = 1 mark.
- You should aim to make relevant points according to the number of marks.
- You should aim to include two or three pieces of relevant information from the source. They must be key points.
- Be careful with this! Not all the information in the source will help you answer the question. Some information may not be relevant to the question.

In order to successfully complete the answer:

- Be sure only to give information which directly answers the question.
- Once you have used the source you will need to add in information from your own knowledge to help you get full marks. If you only use the source, you cannot get full marks. Likewise, if you only use your own knowledge you risk not getting a good mark.
- You can develop points by giving further information and adding more detail to your point. However, this must be linked to the question.

Example question

Source A is from *Germany 1918–1939* by John Kerr (Pearson Education Limited).

Source A

> In 1923, the Nazis attempted to seize power in Munich and overthrow the Bavarian Government. With the collapse of this Beer Hall Putsch, most people believed that Hitler and the Nazis were finished. But the trial gave Hitler much needed national publicity. He was photographed standing beside General Ludendorff, which made people think Hitler was an important person. When he was found guilty, Hitler was given a short prison sentence.

Describe the results of the 1923 Beer Hall Putsch. **6 marks**

The question is worth 6 marks – so you need six pieces of information describing what happened as a result of the Beer Hall Putsch. You should make points that are included in the source and you must also add further developed points or key points from your own knowledge.

Answer 1

Hitler attempted to seize power in Munich and take over the Bavarian Government. This was called the Beer Hall Putsch. It was when he tried to take power in Germany.

Markers' comments

A marker will look at this answer and give marks for two areas: information which comes from the source (Presented Evidence or PEv) and also the candidate's own information (recalled information or R). After each tick, the marker will put either PEv or R depending on which category this falls into.

This candidate has clearly answered in three sentences. However, all the information has come from the source and the candidate has not added anything from his/her own knowledge. The candidate has copied most of the first sentence and has not attempted to answer the question. Therefore full marks cannot be awarded for this answer.

Answer 2

In 1923 Hitler had tried to take over the government in Bavaria with the Beer Hall Putsch. Many of Hitler's followers were injured or even killed by police marksmen. Hitler failed, but it was not all bad as it helped his cause in the long run. Hitler got some good national publicity and had his photo taken with General Ludendorff, who was a World War I hero. Hitler was sent to jail but even this was a good thing for Hitler. He used the court case to get even more publicity. He also wrote his book 'Mein Kampf' when in prison. This book became important for telling other people about his ideas and getting support for the Nazis. While a failure, the Putsch actually helped Hitler and the Nazis in the long run.

Markers' comments

This scores full marks. The candidate has used the source but has also added in information from his/her own knowledge. Look at the source again and then look at the answer. See if you can find which bits have been taken from the source and which bits the candidate has added in from his/her own knowledge.

Explain question

These questions ask you to explain why an event or change happened. They are worth 5 marks. You will recognise them because they will start with the phrase 'Explain the reasons why …'. There is no set way to answer these questions, but there are some basic rules.

Key points

In order to successfully complete the answer:

- You need to write at least five sentences – one for each mark. Sometimes, it is appropriate to write two paragraphs.
- You get a mark for each point you make relevant to the question. A further mark is available for developing points.
- Each point you make must be linked to the question – there must be a clear link between the information and the issue in question.
- You must do more than just describe the issue/situation/change.

Example question

Explain why Hitler was able to become Chancellor in 1933. **5 marks**

Answer 1

Hitler became Chancellor of Germany in 1933. He was a very good public speaker and was popular across Germany. Hitler would criticise all opponents and used violence to intimidate others. He targeted the Jewish population in Germany and used them as a scapegoat for all Germany's problems. Hitler also hated the Treaty of Versailles and promised revenge for the defeat of the First World War. The Nazis eventually won enough votes to become a large party in the Reichstag.

Markers' comments

Answer 1 is a weak answer despite giving some relevant points. The main issue is that the points are not linked to the question and are simple descriptions. Each point needs to be linked to the question for it to count towards the total. This is a common mistake, as candidates often give factors that relate to the question but without explaining the link to the question. For example, in answer 1 the second sentence could end with '... and this popularity meant that President Hindenburg thought he would be a successful Chancellor.'

Answer 2

Hitler was able to become Chancellor in 1933 because people in the Weimar government were seen as weak and so people turned to more extreme parties like the Nazis for stronger leadership. Hitler's use of propaganda also helped gain supporters. For example, parades and large public meetings excited many and this gained votes. Along with this propaganda, Hitler promised jobs to the unemployed and a creation of a stronger Germany. This encouraged people to vote for him. Ordinary Germans were keen to support the Nazis as many were scared of the influence of the Communists. Nazi anti-Communist and anti-Jewish policies became very popular. Hitler was also able to become Chancellor in 1933 due to the intimidation of others. For those not persuaded by the campaigning, the bullying tactics intimidated many that were reluctant to support. In the short term, Hitler became Chancellor due to the lack of effective alternatives, and so President Hindenburg had little choice.

Markers' comments

Answer 2 is clearly the stronger answer as it links directly to the question and makes relevant points that explain the factors in detail. It does much more than describe the issue.

To what extent? question

This type of question requires you to make a judgement about the extent to which a particular factor contributed to an event or development. You are required to give a balanced answer after making a judgement about the relative importance of other relevant factors and come to a reasoned conclusion.

Key points
- The To what extent? question is allocated 8 marks.
- Up to 5 marks can be gained for relevant points of knowledge. 1 mark will be awarded for each separate correct and relevant point made. However a maximum of 3 marks will be awarded if only one factor is discussed.
- The remaining 3 marks are awarded for the structure of your answer:
  - 1 mark will be awarded if you have structured your answer. This means that if you have made a judgement about the factor in the question and then balanced this with a judgement about the importance of other factors.
  - 1 mark will be awarded for your conclusion or overall judgement and 1 mark will be awarded for providing a reason to support your conclusion.

In order to successfully complete the answer:

- Make a judgement about the importance of the factor identified in the question.
- Balance this with a judgement about the importance of other factors relevant to the question.
- Come to a conclusion or overall judgement based on the points made in your answer.
- Provide a reason or reasons to support your conclusion.

Example question
To what extent was the delay in the abolition of the slave trade due to the effects of the French Revolution?   **8 marks**

Answer 1

The French Revolution was important in delaying the abolition of the slave trade as it turned many people against abolition.

However there were other reasons which played a part in delaying abolition. Abolition was also delayed as there were MPs in parliament who represented plantation owners. These MPs voted against abolition. Other important people also argued against abolition as they thought that the abolition of the slave trade would destroy Britain's empire.

In conclusion the effects of the French Revolution were important in delaying the abolition of the slave trade.

Markers' comments

The answer begins with a judgement about the extent to which the effects of the French Revolution contributed to the delay of abolition. A brief point of knowledge (that the French Revolution resulted in a decline in the popularity of the abolitionist campaign) is given in support of the judgement. The answer is structured (with the word 'However…') and proceeds to provide two points of knowledge in support of other factors. The answer ends with a conclusion but not a reasoned conclusion. In other words, no reason or explanation is given in support of the conclusion. This answer has both strengths and weaknesses. It provides a balanced assessment of the factors which contributed to the delay of abolition. However there are not enough relevant key points of knowledge given to gain 5 marks. This answer would instead gain 3 marks for knowledge. The answer is structured with a conclusion but no reason is provided in support of the conclusion. This answer would gain 2 marks out of a possible 3 for structure. Overall this answer would gain 5 marks out of 8.

Answer 2

It is believed that the abolition of the slave trade was delayed due to the events of the French Revolution. The execution of Louis XVI led to the British government passing Acts against large political meetings which meant it was difficult for abolitionists to meet. As a result there was a temporary decline in support for the abolitionist movement.

However there were other reasons why the abolition of the slave trade was delayed. An important obstacle was the fact that the slave trade was profitable and brought huge wealth to Britain through trade and taxes. Furthermore, powerful groups such as MPs, planters and merchants from cities such as London, Liverpool and Bristol also defended the slave trade. Lastly, it is believed that another reason for the delay in the abolition of the slave trade was the slave rebellion on Saint Domingue which exaggerated the fear of slave revolts and violence which discredited arguments in favour of abolition.

Overall the impact of the French Revolution was an important reason for the delay of abolition. It led to a decline in support for the abolition movement, among both the British people and MPs.

Markers' comments

This answer begins by making a judgement about the importance of the factor (the effects of the French Revolution) identified in the question. Two points of knowledge are given in support of this judgement. The answer is then structured and balanced with a consideration of the importance of other factors. Three distinct relevant reasons are given to further explain the delay in abolition. The answer concludes with an overall judgement and a reason is given to support this overall conclusion. This is a strong answer which would gain 5 marks for knowledge, 1 mark for providing a structured account, 1 mark for a conclusion and 1 mark for providing a reason in support of the conclusion. This answer would therefore be awarded the full 8 marks.

Evaluate the usefulness of a source

This question requires you to evaluate whether a source is useful for helping you learn about an event or period in history.

Key points

In order to successfully complete the answer you must comment on:

- **Provenance**

  This means **who** produced the source, **when** the source was produced, and **why** the source was produced.

  In the exam there is up to 3 marks available for this section.

  *In order to gain marks for the section on Provenance it is not enough to simply identify who wrote it, when it was written or why it was written. You must include an **evaluative comment**. In other words you must make a comment on how these things affect the usefulness of the source.*

- **Content**

  This means **what** the source tells you.

  In the exam there is up to 3 marks available for this section.

- **Content omission**

  This means what the source **does not tell you.**

  It is important that you use **specific recall** to illustrate content omission.

  In the exam there is up to 3 marks available for this section.

Example question

Source A is a report from the Moscow municipal corporation describing tenement buildings in the city written in 1902.

> The apartment has a terrible appearance, the plaster is crumbling, there are holes in the walls, stopped up with rags. It is dirty. The stove has collapsed. Legions of cockroaches and bugs. No double window frames and so it is piercingly cold. The lavatory is so dilapidated that it is dangerous to enter and children are not allowed in. All apartments in the house are similar.

Evaluate the usefulness of **Source A** as evidence of the living conditions of workers in Russia during the Tsar's reign.   **6 marks**

(You may want to comment on who wrote it, when they wrote it, why they wrote it, what they say or what has been missed out.)

Answer 1

> *Source A is quite useful. It is a primary source from 1902. It is an extract from a report by the Moscow municipal corporation. It was written to tell us that the stove has collapsed. The source tells us that the lavatory was dangerous and there were no double framed windows so it was cold. It does not tell us what would happen to children if they went into the lavatory.*

Markers' comments

Answer 1 makes some very common mistakes which you must try to avoid.

- It fails to use the language of the question. You must use the language of the question to show the marker that you are engaging with the question.

- In the comments on provenance it does not give evaluative comments. It would receive no marks for provenance because of this.

- It has confused purpose with content.

- It has not given a piece of specific recall for content omission.

Answer 2

> *Source A is only partly useful as evidence of the living conditions of workers in Russia during the Tsar's reign. It is a primary source from 1902 when the Tsar was in power: this is useful because it is from the time period we are being asked about. It is an extract from a report by the Moscow municipal corporation: this makes it useful because it is an official document and is part of a report into housing conditions. It is therefore likely to be accurate and not affected by bias. The purpose of the source is to provide an accurate report on the state of tenement housing in Moscow so is likely to be trustworthy.*

The source is useful to us as evidence of the living conditions of workers because it provides very detailed examples of how the tenements in Moscow were dangerous and unpleasant places to live. For example it tells us that they are in a bad condition; 'the plaster is crumbling'. It also tells us that they are dangerous; 'The lavatory is so dilapidated that it is dangerous to enter and children are not allowed in.' It also tells us that the tenements are unhygienic; 'Legions of cockroaches and bugs.'

The source is not totally useful however as there are some things which the source does not tell us. It does not tell us that some workers lived in barracks that were built right beside the factory. In these barracks families were overcrowded and people on different shifts even had to share beds. The source is also limited because it only tells us about Moscow, it does not tell us about other cities in Russia.

Overall therefore the source is only partly useful as evidence of the living conditions of workers

Markers' comments

Answer 2 is obviously a much more successful answer than answer 1. It constantly uses the language of the question, and an evaluative comment is added to every point.

Source comparison question

This question requires you to compare the views of two sources overall and in detail.

Key points
- The question is worth 4 marks.

In order to successfully complete the answer:
- When comparing the sources overall you must describe what they agree or disagree about without quoting. There are up to 2 marks available for overall comparisons.
- When comparing the sources in detail you must use specific examples supported by quotations. There are up to 2 marks available for direct comparisons.

Example question

Source A describes the Battle of Loos.

> The Battle of Loos was fought in September 1915. On September 25th the British 1st Army commanded by Douglas Haig attacked German positions at Loos. Haig's plan was simple – concentrated British artillery fire and pinpoint infantry fire would give the advancing British troops sufficient cover. In the lead up to the attack, another weapon became available to Haig – poison gas. He realised that such a weapon would neutralise the German machine gunners. The British lost many men to German machine gun fire as they attacked German positions around Loos without the aid of artillery support. The battle effectively ended on September 28th. The British suffered 50 000 casualties while the Germans lost about 25 000 men.

[Adapted from http://www.historylearningsite.co.uk/battle_of_loos.htm]

Source B describes the Battle of Loos.

The Battle of Loos formed a part of the wider Artois-Loos Offensive conducted by the French and British in autumn 1915. Presided over by Douglas Haig, the British committed six divisions to the attack. Haig's battle plans called for the release of 5100 cylinders of chlorine gas from the British front line. During the battle the British suffered 50 000 casualties. German casualties were estimated much lower, at approximately half the British total. The British failure at Loos contributed to Haig's replacement of French as Commander-in-Chief at the close of 1915.

[Adapted from http://www.firstworldwar.com/battles/loos.htm]

Compare the views of Sources A and B on the Battle of Loos.   **4 marks**

Answer 1

The sources agree. They are both describing the Battle of Loos. Source A says it was fought in autumn 1915 and Source B says it was in September 1915. Source A says that they used poison gas and source B says they used chlorine gas. Both sources say that the British lost 50 000 men.

Markers' comments

Answer 1 is very basic in its approach. The overall comparison does not describe the views of the sources, only what they describe. It does not use the language of the question and it offers basic comparisons without developing the point.

Answer 2

Sources A and B agree about the Battle of Loos. The sources agree that the British were commanded by Douglas Haig and agree about the tactics he used during the battle. They also agree that the British suffered heavy losses during the battle.

The sources agree that the battle took place in autumn 1915. Source A writes 'The Battle of Loos was fought in 1915', Source B agrees by writing 'The Battle of Loos formed a part of the wider Artois-Loos Offensive conducted by the French and British in autumn 1915.' The sources further agree that the British were commanded by Douglas Haig: Source A states 'the British 1st Army commanded by Douglas Haig attacked German positions at Loos' and Source B agrees by writing 'Presided over by Douglas Haig, the British committed six divisions to the attack'. The sources also agree that Haig used poison gas: Source A writes 'In the lead up to the attack, another weapon became available to Haig – poison gas' and source B writes 'Haig's battle plans called for the release of 5100 cylinders of chlorine gas from the British front line'. The sources also agree that the British suffered much heavier losses than the Germans. Source A writes 'The British suffered 50 000 casualties while the Germans lost about 25 000 men' and source B agrees by writing 'During the battle the British suffered 50 000 casualties. German casualties were estimated much lower, at approximately half the British total.'

Markers' comments

Answer 2 is much more successful than answer 1. It consistently uses the language of the question and successfully compares the source overall and in detail. When it gives direct comparisons it develops the point by stating what they agree about, and then quotes to support the point.

How fully does source? question

This question requires you to make a judgement about the extent to which a source provides a full explanation or description of an event or development.

Key points

- A How fully? question will ask 'How fully does source ... explain ...?' or 'How fully does source ... describe ...?'

- The source you are asked to evaluate will contain four points relevant to the question but the source will also contain information which is not relevant to the question. It is important that you read both the question and source carefully.

- A How fully? question will be allocated either 5 or 6 marks. A maximum of 3 marks can be gained from identifying and interpreting points from the source. The remaining marks can be gained by adding points from your own knowledge. A maximum of 4 marks can be gained from adding your own knowledge. This of course adds up to 7 marks. This however means that you can gain full marks in different ways. If the question is worth 5 marks you could earn 3 source marks and 2 knowledge marks or you could earn 2 source marks and 3 knowledge marks, for example. Likewise if the question is worth 6 marks you could gain 2 source points and 4 knowledge marks. However a maximum of 2 marks will be awarded for answers which do not contain a judgement. Likewise, answers which refer only to the source will also only be awarded 2 marks.

In order to successfully complete the answer:

- Read the source carefully and make a judgement about how fully the source describes/explains the event or development in the question. For example, **The source describes/explains ... quite well.**

- Identify and interpret what the source tells you about the event or development. For example, **The source states that ...**

- Identify what important information the source does **not** mention. For example, **The source, however, does not mention that ...**

Example question

Source A is about some of the problems facing Mary, Queen of Scots in 1561 and is adapted from *The Kings and Queens of Scotland* by Richard Oram (The History Press).

> Mary's welcome lasted for several days with music and merrymaking. Most were delighted to have their young queen back to rule in person. However some Scots doubted Mary's ability to rule due to her youth and lack of experience. A minority of leading religious reformers including John Knox feared that Mary's return would upset the progress of the Scottish Reformation. Her insistence in maintaining her Catholic faith had to be explained. Mary also had to concede to the wishes of those Scots who now worshipped in the Protestant manner.

How fully does Source A describe the problems Mary, Queen of Scots faced when she arrived in Scotland in 1561?

Answer 1

Source A says that some Scots doubted Mary's ability to rule as she was young and did not have a lot of experience in governing a country. The source states that Protestant leaders like John Knox did not trust Mary and thought she would try to put an end to the Scottish Reformation. The source also says her insistence in maintaining her Catholic faith had to be explained. Mary also had to concede to the wishes of those Scots who now worshipped in the Protestant manner.

Markers' comments

Answer 1 contains no judgement about how fully the source describes the problems facing Mary in 1561. Four points have been identified from the source. These four points are all relevant to the question. However, only the first two points have been interpreted. The other two points have merely been copied. No points of omission have been included. Due to the answer only referring to the source and the lack of a judgement, 2 marks only would be given for this.

Answer 2

Source A partly describes the problems facing Mary, Queen of Scots on her return to Scotland in 1561. Source A mentions how some Scots did not believe Mary could rule Scotland properly due to the fact she was young and inexperienced. The source also mentions how Protestant reformers such as John Knox did not welcome Mary's return to Scotland as they were worried she would interfere with the Protestant Reformation. The source also states how Mary insisted on worshipping the Catholic religion when Scotland had become a Protestant country. However Source A does not mention that some Scots were suspicious that Mary had been brought up in France and the French were unpopular with many Scots. Another important point not mentioned in Source A is that Mary now ruled over a religiously divided country. While Protestants did not want Mary to undo the Reformation, Catholics hoped Mary would restore the Catholic faith. Lastly, another problem facing Mary not mentioned in the source is that Elizabeth of England was suspicious of Mary after Mary claimed to be Queen of England.

Markers' comments

Answer 2 is a much stronger answer. There is a clear overall judgement at the beginning of the answer as to how fully the source describes the problems facing Mary, Queen of Scots in 1561. Three problems facing Mary are identified from the source. Each point is dealt with separately. These points are interpreted rather than simply being copied or listed from the source. There is therefore an understanding of the points being selected to support the judgement made at the beginning of the answer. In addition three good points of knowledge are made to support the candidate's judgement. This is a good answer which would gain full marks.

Added value unit

The assignment – background information

What is the added value unit?

The added value unit is an **assignment** you will need to complete as part of your History course work.

In total there are 80 marks available to you in History. In the exam there are 60 marks available and in the assignment there are 20.

The assignment makes up 25% of your overall mark so it is vital that you do well in it.

Assignment
20 marks

25%

75%

Exam
60 marks

The assignment tests your skills, knowledge and understanding. The assignment also gives you a chance to be challenged and to apply your skills and knowledge.

The best part of this assignment is that you get to choose your own topics to research and write about.

Your teacher can advise you on questions but cannot pick one for you. This is your piece of work.

What do I need to do?

You will get up to eight hours to choose a topic and question, plan out your assignment and also do your research.

At the end of this time you need to gather all your thoughts on to a single page of A4. This is your History Resource Sheet.

You will take this sheet into a room with you where, under controlled exam conditions, you will be given one hour to write up your assignment as an essay.

You can write as much as you want (or can) in the hour. There is no minimum or maximum word limit.

So what do I do now?

Choose a topic you have been studying which you have enjoyed and would like to find out more about. Decide on a historical issue or question. It is all very well liking a topic but real history is about questioning, debating and analysing. So you will need to come up with a question.

This might seem quite hard but there is help at hand. Look at sample or old exam papers for the essay questions. These questions are ones which the SQA have approved so they are good questions to use.

You can choose any question you like but it might be a good idea to choose a question on one of the topics you have been studying as it will deepen your knowledge before the exam.

Good questions and ones to avoid

☒ Lenin and the Russian Revolution

This is not a question but just a topic area. Any essay would be a story and not a historical analysis.

☒ To what extent did the use of gas at the Battle of Loos reduce the confidence of Scottish soldiers in gas as a weapon for the rest of the Great War?

This is a historical question but it is very detailed and is one which you might struggle to find source material to write a whole essay on.

✗   Was the Gestapo Hitler's most effective instrument of terror and how did he get into power?

This is a two-part question and makes it difficult for you as you would be trying to answer two questions at the same time.

✓   How far can it be argued that Martin Luther King was responsible for securing the 1968 Civil Rights Act?

This is an ideal question as you can mention Martin Luther King's contribution and also bring in other factors like Malcolm X's contribution, the Black Panthers, politicians' influence and other factors.

Some other good questions could include:

✓   How significant was Mary's marriage to Bothwell in leading to her downfall?

✓   To what extent was the potato famine of the 1840s the main reason for Irish immigration to Scotland in the 19th century?

✓   How far can it be argued that the First World War improved the economy of Scotland?

✓   How significant was the work of the colonial government in explaining the reasons for Scottish emigration in the 19th century?

✓   To what extent was the effect of the French Revolution the main reason for the delay in the abolition of the slave trade?

✓   How important was the Royal Commission of 1842 in improving working conditions in the coal mines?

✓   How far can it be argued that the Labour Party successfully created a Welfare State?

✓   How far can it be argued that the personality of the Tsar was the most important reason why there was a revolution in Russia in February 1917?

✓   To what extent do the actions of the Gestapo explain the lack of successful opposition to Nazi control in 1930s Germany?

✓   How far can it be argued that the civil rights campaign under Martin Luther King was unsuccessful?

✓   How important was the role of Gorbachev in changing relations between the Superpowers, 1968–81?

Take a look back at the questions to avoid and what we have said about why they are difficult questions for the assignment. Have a think about how these questions might be improved on. What other questions might you ask about these topics? Jot down some ideas and look at past and sample papers to see if these are the sort of questions that will help you write a good historical analysis essay.

Planning the assignment

You will get to take a one page History Resource Sheet in with you when it is time to write up your assignment.

To help you get to that stage you will need to have a master plan of how you are going to attack your question. You will need to make sure that the question has lots of factors to discuss and analyse. Questions which start with 'To what extent …' or 'How far can it be argued ….' are good. Simple 'describe' questions do not give a chance for debate. For example:

To what extent did the Nazis' rise to power depend on propaganda?

Yes, propaganda

Also, unemployment

Also, appeal of uniform

Also, Nazi promise of employment

Also, conflict with Communists

Also, fear

Also, 'All Things to All Men'

For each question there will be a number of different areas you will want to explore as the diagram above shows. You will need to gather evidence under each area and will want to use different sources to gather that evidence. Each piece of evidence helps to **attack your question**.

You must use at least two different sources when you are researching the assignment.

To help gather all your research you might want to put together a folder with poly pockets or a sheet of paper for each factor you are going to explore. You can then write notes on each sheet or drop notes and post-its into the poly pocket.

Source checklist
- your jotter
- class textbooks
- library books
- ebooks
- websites
- TV documentaries
- history magazines
- local historians
- local sites, e.g. castles

Remember to take a note of which source you got each piece of information from (even if you put it in brackets after your notes). This is good practice to get into and you can mention in your essay where you got information from.

Propaganda

'All Things to All Men'

Unemployment

Conflict with Communists

Appeal of uniform

Nazi promise of employment

Fear

Hitler's personality

TOP TIP

Use as much of the single page of A4 History Resource Sheet as possible. For example, don't write Winston Spencer Churchill, simply write WSC. World War One can be shortened to WW1. Try to use the History Resource Sheet to outline your essay paragraphs and issues. You might also use it for quotes, statistics, dates or key names you might forget.

The structure of the assignment

Your added value unit should look like an essay with an introduction, paragraphs on each factor in your essay and a conclusion. The illustration below shows the sort of structure it might take.

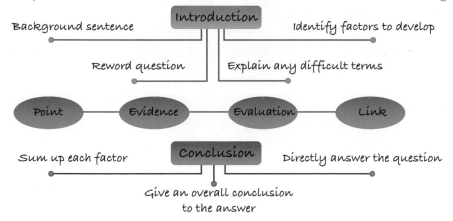

Background sentence — Introduction — Identify factors to develop

Reword question — Explain any difficult terms

Point — Evidence — Evaluation — Link

Sum up each factor — Conclusion — Directly answer the question

Give an overall conclusion to the answer

The above illustration shows that your introduction must set the question in context, explain terms that need further explanation and then shows all the factors you are going to develop in your essay.

Each paragraph should make a point, then give evidence to back it up. The writer (i.e. you) must then evaluate how important that point and evidence is. You should then write a sentence which links that paragraph back to the main question (almost like a mini conclusion for that section).

The conclusion must give a summary of the evidence, answer the question clearly, summarise each of the factors and use evidence from the main essay.

TOP TIP

Do not finish with a quote. It is your essay – you are the historian. If using quotes then make sure you use them to back up your arguments. Or, better still, argue against quotes of other historians. That is real history!

A checklist to help you

TOP TIP

You should practise writing out your essay four or five times before you do the final write up. This will make the essay familiar to you and get you used to the time restriction.

Did you?	Not done	Done	Done well	Self-assessment/ number of marks
Preparation				
Have I chosen an appropriate question and got it checked by my teacher?				
Have I developed a plan?				
Have I identified more than one source to research?				
Overall structure				
Have I organised information to address the question?				/3
Introduction				
Have I shown that different factors caused an event or development?				/2
Have I used my knowledge to show why a factor is important?				/4
Have I used sources to back up arguments for or against each factor?				/2
Have I evaluated different factors?				/3
Conclusion				
Have I come to conclusion?				/3
Have I used evidence from the essay in my conclusion?				/3

Remember, you will not lose any marks for doing things wrong. Marking is always positive and you will be marked for what you have done well!

Answers to Quick Tests

Mary, Queen of Scots and the Reformation, 1542–1587

Page 9

1. Advised monarchy in the government (Privy Council and Parliament); ruled regions; raised armies and acted as regents.

2. Church was too wealthy; some churchmen held several church positions; church positions given to families of kings and nobles; some monks and nuns did not lead holy lives.

3. Henry VIII made too many demands such as an end to the old alliance, control of Scottish castles and charge of Mary. He seized Scottish ships.

4. For safety. After the Treaty of Greenwich was cancelled, the English attacked Scotland both as punishment and in order to capture Mary (the 'Rough Wooing').

Page 11

1. Martin Luther, George Wishart, John Knox, John Calvin, Andrew Melville.

2. Protestant lords who wanted to establish the Reformation in Scotland.

3. There was resentment of French influence in Scotland; there were protests against the execution of Protestant leaders; the accession of Elizabeth gave encouragement to Protestant leaders.

4. Protestant nobles led by Lord Ruthven kidnapped James VI.

Page 13

1. Some Scots did not want a young female ruler; some Scots were anti-French and resented her French upbringing; Mary was Catholic when Scotland had become Protestant.

2. Mary included her Protestant half-brother, James Stewart, Earl of Moray, in her government. She travelled around Scotland to get to know her subjects. She took action against nobles who challenged her. She did not interfere with the Protestant Reformation.

3. They resented his influence at court; they were jealous of his friendship with Mary; they distrusted him because he was Catholic.

4. Loch Leven Castle.

Page 15

1. A silver casket containing love letters allegedly written by Mary to Bothwell.

2. To make it harder for her supporters to plot to free her.

3. A plot by Sir Anthony Babington, an English Catholic, to free Mary, with Spanish help, murder Elizabeth and restore the Roman Catholic religion to England by placing Mary on the English throne.

4. Mary's death warrant was hidden among a pile of letters requiring Elizabeth's signature.

Answers to Quick Tests

Migration and Empire, 1830s–1939

Page 19

1. Push: unemployment, low wages, religious and political persecution, potato famine. Pull: job opportunities, higher wages, religious and political freedom, close location to Ireland, a port for further migration across the Atlantic.

2. They were skilled workers and did not steal jobs.

3. They were persecuted by the Nazis and many chose to leave central Europe. Scotland was seen as a place of religious freedom.

4. Second city of the Empire.

Page 21

1. There were more of them; they had a different religion; worked for lower wages, so were seen to be stealing jobs; tended to stick to their own communities.

2. Fewer of them; same religion; spoke English; had Scottish sounding surnames.

3. Catholic schools; sports teams.

4. Railways; other transport networks (canals, subway system).

Page 23

1. Farming became less profitable; sheep grazing and shooting estates could make more money; potato famine was a catalyst.

2. Offered financial help to set up missionaries.

3. The government gave money to colonies to support emigration from Scotland.

4. Canada; Australia; New Zealand; USA.

Page 25

1. Place names; pipe bands, Burns clubs, Caledonian societies still in existence.

2. To look for gold.

3. Otago.

4. Imported tea and made it an affordable and fashionable drink in Britain.

The Era of the Great War, 1910–1928

Page 29

1. Out of patriotism; for the excitement of adventure; they believed the propaganda; because of the example of football players; for the opportunity of a steady wage.

2. The war evolved into a stalemate and traditional tactics became obsolete.

3. To bombard the enemy lines with heavy artillery and then send troops 'over the top' to advance on the German trenches.

4. General Douglas Haig.

Page 31

1. A war in which the effects are felt in all aspects of public life at home, not just on foreign battlefields.

2. They filled gaps in the workforce created by conscription of men into the army.

3. Political advertising designed to influence the way that the public thought about the war.

4. Their political or religious beliefs.

Page 33

1. The pre-war decline in industry was reversed and unemployment virtually disappeared.

2. The shipbuilding industry, the jute industry and the munitions industry.

3. The demands created by fighting the war disappeared. Also, the war disrupted trading partnerships and former markets began to look elsewhere for their suppliers.

4. They were centred mainly on the Midlands and the South of England.

Page 35

1. Allowed the government to legislate on everyday aspects of public life.

2. Movement into the city for factory work increased demand for housing. Landlords increased rents and evicted those who could not pay.

3. The government extended the franchise to all men over the age of 21 and 'respectable' women over the age of 30.

4. David Lloyd George promised to build 500 000 new homes to improve living conditions for returning servicemen but because of economic hardship only 213 000 were built.

The Atlantic Slave Trade, 1770–1807

Page 39

1. It involved the enslavement of millions of Africans, it was racist as only Africans were enslaved, and slavery was for life and was inhumane and cruel.

2. Slaves were tightly packed and chained below deck in filthy, unsanitary conditions. Many died from disease.

3. Ships first of all sailed to the west coast of Africa. Ships then carried slaves across the Atlantic to the West Indies and the Americas, before sailing back to Britain with slave-produced goods and raw materials.

4. Guns, alcohol, pots and pans and textiles were traded for slaves. Rum, tobacco, coffee, sugar, molasses and cotton were shipped back to Britain to be sold for profits.

Page 41

1. Liverpool and Bristol

2. Sugar

3. Many British sailors first gained experience on board slave ships.

4. They bought large country estates or built large town houses. Some used their wealth from the slave trade to invest in banks, industries or new businesses.

Page 43

1. Controlled the number of slaves ships could carry and required ships to have a doctor on board.

2. The Quakers and the Methodists.

3. Killed by being thrown overboard.

4. To discourage escape attempts.

Page 45

1. Abolishing slavery would be too difficult as an important part of Britain's wealth depended on products produced by slaves and slave owners might demand compensation.

2. Olaudah Equiano.

3. Plantation owners; MPs who had businesses connected with the slave trade or who had been bribed by plantation owners to vote against abolition bills; cities/ports whose wealth was linked to the slave trade.

4. The abolitionist campaign had a lot of popular support, pro-abolitionist MPs worked tirelessly inside Parliament to get an abolition bill passed, the slave trade was no longer as important to Britain's economy.

Changing Britain, 1760–1900

Page 49

1. Cholera; tuberculosis; typhoid; typhus; scarlet fever; smallpox.

2. People blocked up windows; led to poor ventilation and diseases like tuberculosis.

3. 1855 Nuisance Removal Act; 1875 Artisans' and Labourers' Dwellings Improvement Act.

4. Less overcrowding; facilities shared with fewer people; cleaner water supply; better diet.

Page 51

1. A lung disease caused by breathing in coal dust.

2. Reduced the risk of explosions.

3. It was done while the machinery was in operation; led to many accidents.

4. Crompton's mule; Arkwright's water frame.

Page 53

1. One horse pulling a barge could move more goods than one horse pulling a cart.

2. Railways were cheaper, faster, less affected by weather and could carry more.

3. Inland navigator: men who built the railway networks; often Irish.

4. Brought fresh food into the towns so the diet improved.

Page 55

1. Arrested some protestors; executed leaders; deported others to Australia.

2. 90% of the population was unable to vote; voting was still very corrupt.

3. Universal male suffrage; secret ballot voting system; fairer distribution of seats; payment of MPs; annual elections.

4. Some working class men were able to vote.

The Making of Modern Britain, 1880–1951

Page 59

1. 'Laissez-faire' is the political idea which states that politics should not interfere in the private lives of individuals.

2. The poor hated the work house and saw it only as a last resort; self-help did not take into account the real causes of poverty; charities were not coordinated so missed out many people who were genuinely in need.

3. The amount of money (£1·08 per week) that was needed to afford the basic necessities of life. If a family had less than this amount they were classed as poor.

4. Sickness, old age, unemployment, low wages and large families, not laziness or personal failings as had been previously thought.

Page 61

1. The young, the old, the sick, the unemployed and the low paid.

2. There was a danger that Britain could lose its position as a global superpower if it did not improve the health of its future workforce and 'fighting stock'.

3. Some of the reforms made the problems of poverty worse because they were contributory schemes which reduced wages.

4. Although the reforms did not eradicate poverty, they did bring an end to old *'laissez-faire'* attitudes and made it acceptable for the government to pass laws to help the poor.

Page 63

1. The Second World War changed attitudes to poverty because bombing raids affected both rich and poor and increased support for government intervention. Rationing meant there was an equality of sacrifice, and evacuation showed the extent of the problems of poverty.

2. A welfare state is one in which the government provides care for its citizens from the 'cradle to the grave'.

3. Want, Disease, Squalor, Ignorance and Idleness.

4. Comprehensive, universal, contributory, non means tested and compulsory.

Page 65

1. The National Insurance (Industrial Injuries) Act 1946; the National Insurance Act 1946, the National Assistance Act 1948.

2. Labour's social security reforms did not adjust with inflation and so benefits in 1948 were only 19% of the average wage.

3. The biggest criticism of the NHS was the cost. It cost the government £358 million a year, and only a fifth of this total was raised by taxation.

4. The post-war baby boom years meant that there was an increased demand for housing. In 1951 there were 750 000 fewer homes than were needed.

Red Flag: Russia and the Russian Revolution, 1894–1921

Page 69

1. An autocracy is a country in which the ruler has absolute power.

2. The policy introduced to try and make ethnic minorities conform to Russian standards. They were forced to learn Russian and abandon their own traditions.

3. Workers and peasants endured very hard living and working conditions for very little reward. Many peasants were poor, uneducated and illiterate, and had a low life expectancy. Workers' strikes were defeated by violence.

4. He used the Church, the Okhrana, the Cossacks and his chosen ministers.

Page 71

1. The Kadets, the Socialist Revolutionaries and the Social Democrats.

2. Economic problems, the Russo-Japanese War and outrage over the massacre of Bloody Sunday.

3. The Duma had very little power and the Tsar could dissolve it whenever he liked.

4. Peter Stolypin. He tried to reduce poverty by reforming agriculture and industry.

Page 73

1. Russia suffered terrible defeats and loss of life; the war led to food and fuel shortages in Russian cities.

2. He was seen as a coarse and drunken peasant. Because the Tsar's son's illness was a secret the nobles could not understand why they allowed him to be close to them.

3. They issued Order Number 1 which gave them control of the army, railways and postal services. This meant that if the Provisional Government wanted to do anything they had to get the Soviet's permission first.

4. They had not been elected and so felt that they did not have the authority to make important decisions.

Page 75

1. He argued for a second revolution and issued the April Theses, a document which appealed to the basic needs of the Russian people and called for an end to Russia's involvement in the war.

2. Once the Kornilov revolt had failed the Bolsheviks were armed and looked like the saviours of Petrograd. On the other hand the Provisional Government looked weak and Kerensky was discredited.

3. Lenin withdrew Russia from the war.

4. He planned the October Revolution and then ensured that the Red Army were a disciplined fighting force.

Hitler and Nazi Germany, 1919–1939

Page 79

1. They did not feel solely responsible for starting the war.

2. The German politicians who signed the Treaty of Versailles; the first leaders of the Weimar Republic.

3. Printed more money which meant prices went up.

4. It made the government unpopular as they raised taxes and cut wages and benefits; they were seen as weak and people looked for stronger leadership.

Page 81

1. Weimar looked increasingly weak; some were scared of the rising popularity of the Communists; seemed to offer organisation in a time of chaos.

2. 85.

3. Turned people against the Communists; gave them an excuse to pass emergency laws to suspend freedoms which became the basis for the Nazi police state.

4. Gave him power to pass any laws he liked without consulting the Reichstag.

Page 83

1. SA; SS; Gestapo; People's Courts; propaganda; concentration camps.

2. Ensured that Jews and other groups were no longer citizens of Germany; forbad relationships between Jews and non Jews.

3. Josef Goebbels.

4. He was arrested and put in solitary confinement for seven years.

Page 85

1. Government employed people building hospitals, schools and roads; National Service in the armed forces; sacking Jews and women; rearmament factories.

2. To ensure that there was an army of the future; to prepare boys and girls to be loyal to the Nazi party; to sustain the Nazi regime.

3. The importance of racial purity; looking after the home, motherhood and bringing up children.

4. Military style discipline and obedience was expected; textbooks brainwashed children at any opportunity; boys and girls studied subjects that would allow them to fulfil future roles; the anti-Jewish message was spread.

Free at last, 1918–1968

Page 89

1. White Anglo-Saxon Protestant.

2. Southern and eastern Europe; later from Asia and Africa.

3. Raised awareness of them being outsiders; Italians and Japanese especially faced more hostility. (Also Germans.)

4. De jure is legal, de facto has no legal basis.

Page 91

1. Non-WASP countries; Asia and south and eastern Europe especially.

2. Greater hostility to all things foreign; USA closed its borders to immigration.

3. Lynchings; murder; beatings; arson; stopped blacks from voting.

4. The KKK had many influential members; government may lose votes.

Page 93

1. Victory in the war and victory for civil rights; win the war and win equality.

2. They raised awareness of the violence that continued against black Americans.

3. Non-violent protest: marches, speeches, boycotts, sit-ins, freedom rides.

4. Gave them equal voting rights; ended discrimination at work; desegregated public schools.

Page 95

1. To escape persecution in the south; to find homes and jobs in the north.

2. Los Angeles; Chicago.

3. Separate white and black societies; violent protest.

4. Revealed the extent of the gap between black and white societies.

The Cold War, 1945–1989

Page 99

1. The period of rivalry and suspicion between 1945 and 1989 that threatened armed conflict.

2. A buffer zone of communist countries friendly towards the Soviet Union was created.

3. The Berlin Airlift.

4. To protect Western countries from an attack by the Soviet Union.

Page 101

1. Nikita Khrushchev.

2. Hungary's leader Imre Nagy announced that Hungary planned to leave the Warsaw Pact. To put an end to the uprising.

3. To stop East Germans moving to the West through Berlin.

4. The USA imposed a blockage of Cuba, threatened that an attack from Cuba would result in war between the USA and the Soviet Union and mobilised troops for an invasion of Cuba.

Page 103

1. The belief that if one country fell to communism, other countries would also fall to communism, resulting in communism spreading throughout South East Asia.

2. A supply route from North Vietnam to South Vietnam through the neighbouring countries of Laos and Cambodia.

3. They were young, inexperienced and lacked training in jungle warfare and guerrilla tactics.

4. The war was costing billions of dollars; there were large numbers of American casualties; the war was televised and shocked the American people.

Page 105

1. An understanding, a relaxing of tension between the superpowers.

2. SALT I led to a reduction of nuclear weapons; the Helsinki Agreement led to an agreement on European borders; trade links were established between the Soviet Union and the USA; joint space missions.

3. Ronald Reagan.

4. Glasnost and perestroika.